The Stories We Don't Tell

GNANAMBIKAI DEVI R

The Stories We Don't Tell

Made with ❤ on the Notion Press Platform

www.notionpress.com

For Vibha

for whom I'm trying to grow, improve, and live meaningfully.

She's the one who keeps me grounded in this world.

For Prabu

who challenges me to discover my strength

and inspires me to stay positive and adaptable

through everything life brings.

For my brother

who annoys me only because he cares a little too much.

For my parents

with gratitude for their blessings that continue to guide my steps.

CONTENTS

Contents

CONTENTS

Acknowledgements

Writing this book has been a quiet, meaningful journey, and I am grateful to everyone who supported me along the way.

To the people who trusted me with their stories, thank you. Your courage, honesty, and vulnerability shaped every page. Even though the details have been changed to protect your privacy, the emotional truth you shared has guided the heart of this book.

To my mentors and the psychological thinkers whose work has inspired me, thank you for reminding me that compassion is the foundation of every healing space.

To Prabu, thank you for your thoughtful aesthetic ideas, your creative suggestions that helped shape the feel of this book, and for being the first reviewer whose insights offered me a fresh, honest third perspective. Your support added a clarity and confidence I truly needed.

To the digital tools that made this process smoother, especially ChatGPT, thank you for helping me refine my writing, organise my thoughts, and hold space for these stories through every draft.

To everyone who works in the field of mental health, your dedication brings light into places where people have long sat in silence.

And finally, to every reader holding this book, thank you for opening your heart to these stories. May you find comfort, clarity, and hope in these pages, and may you always remember that healing is possible, one gentle step at a time.

ACKNOWLEDGEMENTS

Preface

This book is born from hundreds of voices I have listened to over the years. Voices of joy and struggle, courage and confusion, voices of people doing the best they can with the life they were given.

The details of each journey are unique, yet the roots often feel familiar. We carry childhood memories, family expectations, work pressures, social judgments, and the quiet longing to be seen for who we truly are.

Across countless counselling sessions, I discovered something deeply moving. Most people are not broken. They are learning, growing, healing, trying, and doing the best they can with the emotional tools available to them at the time.

This book is for anyone who has ever felt tired from carrying too much, unsure about love, overwhelmed by expectations, shaped by old wounds, quietly strong despite self-doubt, or simply longing for clarity and peace.

These stories remind us that pain wears many faces, but so does resilience, and so does hope.

My intention is for this book to become a gentle companion for those rebuilding themselves, for those searching for meaning, and for therapists, counsellors, and helpers who wish to hold space with greater kindness and understanding.

Each chapter reflects the importance of emotional safety, compassion, and trauma-informed communication, not just as skills, but as ways of being that help us nurture healthier relationships, kinder families, and more supportive communities.

When we learn to speak with empathy, listen without defensiveness, and respond without harm, we begin to heal spaces that may have been hurting for years.

These stories may remind you of someone you know. They may remind you of yourself. They may help you name feelings you never had the words for.

All stories in this book are written with complete anonymity. Details have been changed and identities protected. This book does not point to any individual; it reflects the shared human experience we all carry within us.

If there is one truth, I hope you take from these pages, it is this: healing is possible, understanding is possible, and hope is possible. And every heart, including yours, deserves all three.

Gnanambikai Devi R

Date: 15-Dec-25

Therapy Room Note

The therapy room is simple,
A soft chair.
A wooden table with a warm lamp.
A box of tissues that never asks questions.
And a quietness rarely found anywhere else.

The chair across from mine is intentionally comfortable a place where people can sink without disappearing. The light is gentle, never harsh, softening edges and making tears less lonely.

When someone enters, the room shifts, not physically, but emotionally.
Every story brings its own temperature.
Some days, the air feels heavy with unspoken grief.
Some days, tense with anger waiting for years.
Some days, silent with numbness from forgotten safety.
And some days, filled with the quiet strength of someone who doesn't yet know they are healing.

But the therapy room is never about the furniture.
It is about the permission it gives.
Permission to slow down.
Permission to let go.
Permission to feel.
Permission to finally speak what has been held inside too long.

When a client sits in that chair, something subtle happens.
Shoulders ease.
Breath softens.
Hands unclench.
Eyes adjust to a silence that accepts without expectation.

Sometimes, they talk.
Sometimes, they cry.
Sometimes, they sit in stillness, gathering courage.
Sometimes, they say a sentence that changes everything.

This room has held anger, guilt, loneliness, heartbreak, trauma, shame, hope, and resilience.

It has witnessed people who thought they were weak discover their strength.

It has witnessed people who thought they had no voice finally hear themselves.

Nothing dramatic happens here only truth.
Two people, Two chairs.
One carrying pain.
One holding space.

If there is anything sacred about this room, it is not the decor.
It is the courage that walks in, and the relief that walks out.

As you enter the chapters of this book, I hope you feel a little of this room, its stillness, its safety, its softness.

You do not have to rush.
You do not have to be perfect.
You do not have to pretend.
Just like every person who has sat in that chair,

"You are welcome here, exactly as you are."

Author's Note

When I first began this work, I believed my role was to guide people.
Over the years, I discovered something deeper,
every person who sat across from me has guided me too.
Their courage shaped my understanding.
Their honesty shaped my compassion.
Their pain shaped my purpose.

This book is not written *about* people it is written *for* people.
For anyone who has carried fear silently.
For anyone who has questioned their worth.
For anyone who has been misunderstood.
For anyone who has been strong for too long.

The chapters that follow belong to no single individual.
They are woven from patterns I have witnessed, emotions I have held, and moments I will never forget.

To protect privacy, details have been altered, identities disguised, and timelines shifted,
but the emotional truth remains untouched.

My intention is not to give perfect answers,
but to offer understanding
the most powerful ingredient in healing.

Therapy taught me that transformation rarely looks dramatic.
It looks like someone showing up to a session they almost cancelled.
It looks like a person admitting a feeling they have hidden for

years.
It looks like a single honest sentence:
"I want to feel better."

If you carry pain while reading this book, I hope these stories make you feel less alone.
If you are supporting someone in pain, I hope they teach you gentler ways to listen.

If you are a therapist, I hope they deepen your respect for the human heart.

Thank you for opening these pages,
Thank you for giving these stories a place to land,
and
thank you, truly, for choosing healing even if it is slow, even if it is messy, even if it is just one small step today.

You deserve a life that feels kind to you.

May this book walk beside you on that journey.

BECAUSE

EVERY HEART

HAS

A STORY

CHAPTER ONE

The Wounds You Cannot Show

She did not enter the room with confidence. She slipped in quietly, as though she hoped not to disturb the air around her. Her smile was small and almost apologetic, the kind worn by people who have learned to hide their pain well.

"Madam… can I sit?" she asked softly, even though the chair was already waiting for her.

There was a trembling calmness about her, the kind that comes from years of surviving rather than living. She adjusted the edge of her dupatta twice before speaking, as if preparing her heart for the weight of what it carried.

"I don't know where to begin," she whispered, and yet, that sentence was enough. It spoke of a story held in silence for too long, a story that needed space, safety, and a little courage to finally unfold.

She began hesitantly.
"I got divorced recently. I have a son… he's still very young."

The words sounded simple, but the life behind them was anything but. Her marriage had been an unending storm of physical abuse, emotional cruelty, and moments that left her feeling ashamed, trapped, and invisible.

The pain did not come only from what her husband did, but also from what her parents failed to do. Each time she reached out for help, she was told to adjust, to stay quiet, to think about the family name. Slowly, the girl inside her learned that her suffering did not matter.

Twice, she tried to hurt herself. Not because she wanted to die, but because she wanted the pain to stop. There were nights when thoughts arose that frightened her.

"If he died," she admitted softly, "maybe my parents would finally accept me."

That thought was not cruelty. It was despair.

Over time, her emotions grew numb. Even motherhood began to feel frightening.
"There were moments," she said, her voice barely steady, "when I felt so unstable that I was scared I might hurt my child."

She loved her son deeply. That was why she left him in her parents' care. Not because she did not want him, but because she did not want him to witness her breaking.

She filed for divorce quietly. It was only after she discovered her husband's hidden truth, his sexuality, that he agreed to a mutual consent divorce. When it was over, she finally told her parents everything, hoping for understanding.

Instead, she was met with anger.

They shouted.
They blamed her again.
They told her not to come home.

In many families, silence is taught as loyalty, and endurance is mistaken for strength, even when it leaves someone alone with unbearable pain.

Now she lived alone in a hostel, working through the day, waking up to silence, and falling asleep with tears no one saw.

"Nights are the worst," she whispered.
"I feel a weight on my chest. I can't breathe. I don't know what I'm living for."

In her loneliness, she reached out to someone from her past. He was married, but he promised to take care of her. To someone emotionally starved, those words felt like water.

She did not expect commitment. She only wanted someone to listen when the heaviness returned, someone who might visit when he was in her city. But slowly, the truth became clear. He wanted money. He grew angry when she could not give it. He disappeared when she needed support and returned only when it suited him.

"Sometimes I think he's cheating me," she said.
"But other times… I convince myself he's a good person."

Her voice carried years of unspoken pain, years of placing others before herself, years of believing she was unworthy of love. Trauma does not attach us to people; it attaches us to familiarity. When harm repeats often enough, the nervous system learns to mistake endurance for safety.

I spoke gently, careful not to rush her understanding.

"What you are experiencing is not weakness," I said. "This is what emotional trauma does. When someone lives in pain for too long, pain begins to feel normal. The nervous system learns to defend what is familiar, even when it hurts. You start believing that love must be earned, endured, or sacrificed for."

When fear has shaped a person's life for years, unfamiliar kindness can feel unsafe. Loneliness feels unbearable, yet conflict feels terrifying. Love becomes something that costs the self.

None of these patterns were her fault. They were scars formed through survival.

"For a long time," I continued, "others decided your life for you. For the first time, you are allowed to ask yourself a different question. What do you deserve?"

Her shoulders loosened slightly, as though a small weight had lifted.

"Maybe," she whispered, "I want to live differently."

That single sentence marked a quiet turning point. Healing does not begin with grand decisions. It begins when the heart allows the possibility that something better might exist.

Her story is not rare. Many survivors of trauma carry loneliness, guilt, fear of boundaries, and confusion about what love should feel like. Silence often feels heavier than words, and when voices are swallowed for too long, the body learns to carry unspoken pain.

Healing begins when language is given to what was hidden, when quiet suffering is allowed to become gentle expression. From there, the journey continues through small, compassionate steps.

The practices that follow are not tasks to complete or goals to achieve. They are gentle invitations. Take what feels right. Leave what feels heavy. Healing moves at the pace of safety, not force.

HEALING PRACTICES

For Loneliness, Fear & Confusion

1. Soothing the Heart Through Breath

Begin with the body, because the body learned fear long before words existed.

Place one hand gently over your heart.
Breathe in slowly for two seconds.
Breathe out for four seconds.

There is no need to count perfectly. Let your breath find its own rhythm.

Silently remind yourself:
My body is allowed to relax. I am not in danger right now.

2. Self-Forgiveness for Survival

Staying. Leaving. Freezing. Breaking down. Becoming numb. These were not failures. They were ways your system tried to protect you.

Survival responses are not choices made from freedom; they are choices made from limited safety.

Gently repeat:
I did what I could with the safety I had.

3. Rebuilding Emotional Safety

Trauma often teaches us to ignore our own needs. Begin by listening again.

Ask yourself, slowly and honestly:
What makes me feel safe?
What makes me feel respected?
What makes me feel seen?
What makes me feel valued?

There are no right answers. Awareness itself is the beginning of safety.

4. A Trauma Clarity Reminder

If you notice yourself justifying someone who has hurt you, pause.

Quietly remind yourself:
Sometimes my heart clings to what is familiar, even when it is not safe.

This reminder is not meant to shame you. It is meant to bring clarity without judgment.

5. Your Safe Circle

Healing does not happen in isolation.

Identify two or three people who feel emotionally steady or comforting. They do not need to fix you or advise you. Their presence alone matters.

Even one safe connection can soften a heavy journey.

6. A Future-Self Check-In

Ask yourself gently:
What would my healed self-want for me right now?

Often, the answer is simple.
Rest. Peace. Tenderness. Protection.

Let that answer guide one small choice today.

7. Practicing a Small, Honest Boundary

You do not need to explain everything.

Practice saying, just once:
I can't do that right now.

Notice what happens in your body afterward. Relief, even mixed with guilt, is often a sign that a boundary was needed.

8. Dignity Grounding (Three Minutes)

Sit or stand with your feet firmly touching the ground.
Take one slow, steady breath.

Then say quietly to yourself:
My story has been painful, but it has not taken away my strength.

Let that sentence settle before you move on.

9. Gentle Daily Self-Care

Choose one or two each day. Nothing more.

Open a window and let fresh air in.
Step outside and observe the sky for two minutes.
Drink water slowly and mindfully.
Read one page of a book.
Light a candle or play soft music.
Take a warm shower.
Sit quietly for two minutes without your phone.

These are not small things. They are acts of repair.

10. Reclaiming Self-Worth

When you feel ready, write down:

What I admire in myself.
What I survived.
What I achieved despite pain.
The qualities I carry, even now.

Self-worth is not something you earn later. It is something you recover.

Reflective Prompt:

Reflect on one moment today when you stayed silent. Was it protection, or was it suppression?

*****

"The curious paradox is that when I accept myself just as I am, then I can change." **— Carl Rogers**

Healing begins when we stop blaming ourselves and start accepting our emotions with honesty and compassion.

CHAPTER TWO

Steps Beyond Fear

She arrived a little earlier than her appointment, not because she was free, but because she did not want to sit alone with her thoughts any longer.

The moment she stepped in, I noticed how tightly her fingers gripped the strap of her handbag, as though holding on to something familiar might steady the fear inside her.

"Is it okay if I sit a little early?" she asked, her voice low and unsure.

She lowered herself into the chair slowly. Her posture was alert yet fragile, as if part of her mind was still living inside the memory of something frightening. Her eyes scanned the room, the way people do when safety has once been uncertain.

"I'm scared to go back to work," she said quietly.

She paused before continuing.
"I work in a high-risk environment. After a traumatic incident at my workplace… I just can't."

Her voice trembled, but she did not cry. Sometimes fear runs so deep that tears cannot even reach the surface.

"Everyone around me keeps giving positive thoughts," she said after a moment.
"they say accidents can happen anywhere. They tell me not to lose courage. They remind me that even people on the ground face risks. I understand all of it," she added softly, "but my mind just won't listen."

Her job had once been her pride.
The training.
The discipline.
The responsibility.
The life it had given her.

"It's this job that gave me everything," she whispered.
"And still… it's this job that now scares me."

She had taken leave after a viral fever. Physically, she had recovered. Emotionally, she could not bring herself to take the final step of getting medical clearance to rejoin.

"I hesitate even to do that," she admitted.
"Just thinking about rejoining brings the fear back. I feel frozen."

As she spoke, I noticed how tightly she held her hands together, as if trying to keep her courage from slipping away.

"It's not that I want to leave my job," she said earnestly.
"I've worked too hard for this. This career gave me stability. It shaped my identity. But going back to the same environment… it keeps reminding me of the incident. It feels like I'm reliving it all over again."

Her words revealed what trauma often hides beneath fear.
She was not afraid of her job.
She was afraid of the memory.

Fear after trauma is not a warning about the present; it is the body remembering a moment when safety was lost.

"This is not weakness," I said softly.
"This is how trauma works."

She looked at me with surprise, perhaps because she had been expecting encouragement to simply be brave, not understanding.

"When something frightening happens," I continued gently, "the brain begins to connect everything around that moment with danger. The place, the sounds, the uniform, the atmosphere. Even when you are objectively safe, your mind behaves as though the danger is still present."

She closed her eyes briefly, as if something inside her finally felt seen.

"It feels exactly like that," she whispered.
"My body reacts even when nothing is wrong."

Her workplace had become a collection of triggers. The familiar noises. The routines. Even the atmosphere felt heavy, as though it carried memories, she was not ready to face.

"I can't concentrate," she said.
"I keep imagining the worst. And then I feel guilty for being scared. I feel like I'm failing myself."

"You're not failing," I replied gently.
"You're healing."

I guided her toward something simple, something the body could understand.

"Place your hand on your stomach," I said softly.
"Breathe with me. Two seconds in. Four seconds out."

At first, her breath wavered. Fear lived close to her chest. But after a few rounds, her shoulders softened slightly.

"Your body has lived in fear for a while," I explained.
"So even safety feels unfamiliar. But the body can relearn. Slowly."

A single tear slipped down her face, not from sadness, but from relief. Someone had finally understood her fear instead of dismissing it.

We spoke about rebuilding comfort in small, respectful steps. Not forcing confidence but gently teaching the nervous system that it was safe again. Beginning with thinking about the workplace calmly. Then looking at related images without pressure. Visiting nearby for a brief moment. Entering the building for just a few minutes. Requesting a phased return, if possible.

"You don't have to rush," I told her.
"You don't have to conquer everything in one day. You can return slowly, one small exposure at a time."

She nodded, her expression carrying a fragile sense of possibility.

"I want to try," she whispered.
"Slowly… but I want to try."

That single sentence held all the strength she thought she had lost.

Fear had been chasing her, cornering her with worst-case scenarios. But somewhere beneath the fear, a quieter truth was beginning to rise.

She wanted her life back,
And wanting is often the first sign of healing.

Fear does not mean you are incapable.
Fear means your body remembers something it once survived.

You do not have to silence fear. You only have to walk past it gently, one small step at a time.

Courage is not always loud.
Sometimes courage is a quiet breath inside a shaking body.

You survived the incident.
You survived the fear.
And now, slowly, you will reclaim the life and the skies that once belonged to you.

Fear after trauma is not imagination. It is the body remembering something it once survived.

The practices given below are not meant to erase fear, but to help your nervous system feel safe enough to move forward, gently and at your own pace.

Take what feels supportive. Leave what feels heavy.

HEALING PRACTICES

For Fear, Panic, and Trauma After a Frightening Event

1. The Grounding Breath

When your mind races or your chest feels heavy, begin with the body.

Place one hand on your stomach.
Breathe in slowly for two seconds.
Breathe out for four seconds.

Repeat this five times, without forcing the breath.

Quietly remind yourself:
My body is learning to calm down.

2. The "Fear or Memory?" Question

When fear rises, pause for a moment and ask yourself gently:

Is this danger happening right now, or is this my body remembering what once happened?

This question is not meant to dismiss fear. It is meant to bring clarity without judgment.

3. Slow and Gentle Exposure

Fear often grows when we avoid what reminds us of the past. Healing happens when we return slowly, with choice and support.

Instead of rushing back into routine, take tiny steps. Move toward the feared situation gradually. Break the return into smaller parts. Allow yourself to pause whenever needed.

Progress measured in kindness is still progress.

4. The Anchor Object

Carry something small that makes you feel supported. It might be a locket, a ring, a bracelet, a keychain, a prayer bead, or even a smooth stone.

When anxiety rises, hold it in your hand and remind yourself:

I am not alone. I am safe.

Let the object become a physical reminder of steadiness.

5. The Reassurance Line

When fear begins to take over, repeat softly, either aloud or in your mind:

I am here. I am safe in this moment. My body is learning to calm down.

Repetition helps the nervous system trust what the mind already knows.

6. Asking for a Gentle Re-entry

When returning to any environment that triggers fear, it is okay to ask for support.

You may request lighter responsibilities. You may build up slowly. You may begin with shorter durations. If possible, surround yourself with someone who feels steady or reassuring.

Needing accommodation is not failure. It is wisdom.

7. Safe Ending Visualization

Spend one quiet minute imagining yourself entering the situation that feels frightening.

Picture yourself doing what is needed.
Picture yourself leaving safely.
Picture the moment you return, feeling relieved, steady, and quietly proud.

Your brain learns safety through repetition, even in imagination.

8. Writing Your "Why"

Write a single line and keep it with you. Somewhere visible. Somewhere reachable.

I have survived before. I can move forward again.

Let this sentence accompany you when fear tries to convince you otherwise.

Reflective Prompt:

Notice one area of your life where fear makes you over-control. What would trust look like instead?

*****

"I am not what happened to me. I am what I choose to become." **— Carl Jung**

Our identity is bigger than our past experiences; we can grow beyond fear and redefine our path.

CHAPTER THREE

Healing Beyond shame

He walked in slowly, as though each step carried hesitation. Not fear of me, but fear of himself. Fear of what he might confess. Fear of how his truth might sound once spoken aloud.

He sat down without waiting for permission, elbows resting on his knees, hands clasped tightly together. His eyes did not meet mine at first. They remained fixed on the floor, as if he were searching for courage in the small cracks between the tiles.

After a long pause, he whispered,
"I messed up again."

When he finally looked up, his eyes were slightly red.

"I don't trust myself anymore," he said.

In that moment, I understood something important. He had not come to explain his addiction. He had come to find himself again.

"I'm addicted to gambling," he said softly.
"It started several years ago with a small amount. I don't even know how it became my whole life."

His voice cracked, not from tears, but from carrying too many secrets for too long.

"At first it was fun," he said.
"But slowly, it became the only thing I could think about."

Gambling had not entered his life loudly. It slipped in quietly, through curiosity, boredom, and the promise of comfort. Then, slowly, it took control. That is how addictions grow. They do not storm the door. They seep through the cracks.

"I took loans," he continued.
"I lied to people I care about.
I got into debts I couldn't handle.
I even sold my inherited property to settle them."

He paused, swallowing a truth that felt sharp.

"That property," he said quietly, "was all I had from my family. I sold it within minutes for gambling money."

There was no anger in his voice. Only shame. Deep, burning, suffocating shame.

"I stopped for a while after that," he said.
"But in three months, I started again."

A family elder had helped him settle his debts a second time.

"He made me promise on my wife and my child," he whispered.
"And still, I broke it."

As he lowered his head, it said more than tears ever could. This was not just shame. This was a man who believed he was beyond repair.

"I lost respect," he said.
"I lost trust. I feel guilty. I feel like I'm not a man anymore. And still, I don't believe in myself. I'm scared that one day I'll lose control again."

He was not afraid of gambling.
He was afraid of himself, or rather, the version of himself that appeared in the grip of addiction.

He took a breath, as though preparing to speak something even heavier.

"And… I'm addicted to self-pleasure. And porn," he said.
"I don't know why I do it. I feel disgusted afterward. But when I try to stop… I can't."

His voice broke for the first time.

It was not the addiction alone that hurt him most. It was the guilt. The shame. The fear that this version of himself would never change. Compulsive behaviours often gather where shame and stress remain unresolved, each one feeding the same need to escape pain.

As he spoke, I could sense the conflict he was trapped within.
He hated what addiction had done to his life.
And he did not know how to believe that he deserved a different one.

Addiction had become both his hiding place and his punishment. Understanding addiction does not excuse the harm it causes, but without understanding, change rarely lasts.

"I want to change," he whispered.
"But I don't trust myself."

I nodded gently.

"Addiction," I said softly, "is not a sign of weakness. It is a sign that your mind has been trying to escape something painful."

He looked at me, confused.

"You didn't gamble because you are bad," I continued. "You gambled because something inside you was hurting."

His eyes softened, as though hope were a language he had not heard in a very long time.

"What you feel now, the guilt, the shame, the fear tells me something important," I said.
"You are still alive inside. People who don't care don't feel guilt. People who want to change feel this pain because addiction is not who they want to be."

He nodded slowly, letting the words settle.

"You relapsed," I said gently.
"That does not mean you failed. Addiction is not a switch you turn off. It is a wound that heals slowly."

Then I offered the first intervention.

"Look at your pattern," I said.
"You stopped after a crisis, then relapsed when life became normal again. This is not a moral issue. This is a brain pattern. We need to break the cycle, not break you."

For the first time, his breath seemed to deepen.

"I'll help you," I said.
"But you must also help yourself. Not by hating yourself, but by understanding yourself."

He nodded again. This time, something had shifted. Not relief. Not confidence. Just the smallest spark of belief.

"I want to try," he whispered.
"I really want to try."

And that was enough.

Healing does not begin with certainty.
Healing begins with willingness.

Addiction is not a sign that you are weak.
It is a sign that you have been hurting in silence.

You are not the worst thing you have ever done.
You are not defined by a relapse.
You are not beyond help.

Recovery is not about becoming perfect.
It is about becoming honest, gentle, and patient with your wounded parts.

If you can feel guilt,
if you can fear losing control,
if you can say, "I want to change,"

then you have already begun healing.

And one day, not too far from now, you will look back and say,

"I didn't defeat the addiction.
I discovered the strength inside me."

His story reminds us that addiction is not a flaw in character, but a response to pain and unmet needs. It grows in silence, where relief feels more urgent than healing. Recovery is not about controlling yourself perfectly, but about learning to pause, understand, and respond differently.

The following practices are meant to support you when urges rise and self-trust feels fragile. Take them slowly. You do not need to master everything at once.

HEALING PRACTICES

For Addiction, Relapse, and Compulsive Habits

1. The Pause-Before-Action Practice

When an urge appears, the goal is not to fight it, but to interrupt it.

Pause.
Take a slow breath.
Name what is happening: *This is an urge.*
Delay acting on it for just five minutes.

Most urges peak and pass if they are not immediately acted upon. Five minutes is often enough to create choice.

2. Shame-Free Reframing

Addiction grows stronger in shame. Healing begins when shame is removed from the conversation.

Gently remind yourself:
This is a pattern, not my identity.
Relapse is a step in recovery, not the end of it.

These statements are not excuses. They are accurate, compassionate truths.

3. Urge Surfing

When an urge feels overwhelming, imagine it as a wave.

It rises.
It peaks.
And it falls.

You do not have to fight the wave. You only have to stay present without acting on it. Every time you ride an urge without giving in, you strengthen your ability to choose.

4. The Accountability Anchor

Recovery is not meant to be done alone.

Choose one safe person to share your progress with. This could be a partner, a counsellor, a trusted friend, or a sibling. The purpose is not to be judged or controlled, but to be gently held accountable.

Secrecy feeds addiction. Safe connection weakens it.

5. Replace, Don't Remove

Addictions rarely disappear through force. They loosen their grip when something healthier takes their place.

When the urge arises, try replacing the behaviour with movement, breath, or connection. A short walk. A cold shower. Music. Journaling. Conscious breathing. Talking to someone. Stepping outside.

Replacement is not distraction. It is redirection.

6. The Urgency Question

When the pull feels strong, pause and ask yourself one honest question:

If I do this now, what will my tomorrow look like?

This question is not meant to scare you. It is meant to reconnect you with your future self.

7. Reducing Access

Willpower alone is rarely enough. Structure matters.

Make relapse harder by removing easy access. This may include deleting gambling apps, blocking websites, limiting cash, moving money into safer accounts, or avoiding high-risk situations.

These are not punishments. They are protective boundaries.

8. The Guilt Reset

Once a day, write or repeat this gently:

My past behaviour was a cry for help.
My new behaviour is a step toward healing.

Guilt keeps you stuck in the past. Compassion helps you move forward.

Reflective Prompt:

Think of one relapse or mistake you carry guilt for. Can you reframe it as part of healing, not failure?

*****

"Unexpressed emotions will never die. They are buried alive and will come forth later in uglier ways."
— Sigmund Freud

When emotions are suppressed instead of understood, they often return through unhealthy behaviours.

CHAPTER FOUR

Trusting Your Body Again

Her bag was still on her shoulder when she spoke.

"Madam… I think something is wrong with me again."

There was no shaking, no tears. Only a subtle tightness around her eyes, the kind that comes from scrolling through symptoms at two in the morning, slowly convincing yourself of the worst.

She sat down with a tiredness that did not come from lack of sleep, but from carrying fear for too long. Her fingers tapped lightly against her lap, as if her body still remembered the hospital bed she had once lain on.

"I was diagnosed with a serious medical infection in March," she began softly.
"I was admitted. They said there was fluid in my stomach, inflammation in my intestines. They even suspected irritable bowel disease."

Her eyes dropped to the floor, as though the memory itself felt heavy to hold.

"They ran so many tests," she said.
"I was scared every minute I was there."

Hospital fear does not fade easily. It lingers in the mind long after the body has healed.

"After I was discharged and my fever was gone, I should have felt normal," she continued.

She swallowed.

"But I couldn't. I kept thinking about the results. I Googled everything. The more I read, the more terrified I became."

Her voice grew softer.

"To rule out IBD, I did a colonoscopy. It came back negative. I felt relieved."

She paused then, a pause filled with the truth she was still living with.

"It's almost been a year," she whispered.
"But I still can't go back to normal. The fear is still inside me. Whenever I hear about someone's illness, or someone's death, even if someone in my family gets a small fever, my mind starts swirling. It goes straight into panic. I can't stop the thoughts. My body reacts like something terrible is happening to me."

Her words trembled.

"Even simple health-related words trigger me. My mind reacts without my permission."

This was no longer just fear. It was the mind replaying trauma again and again from a time when uncertainty felt like danger. Health anxiety is not imagination; it is the nervous system staying alert after a moment when the body did not feel safe.

"Last week, I couldn't sleep," she said.
"And that one night brought everything back. The hospital. The tests. The fear. I felt like something was wrong again."

She touched her stomach unconsciously, checking.

"I keep thinking the fluid might have come back. And now I want to do another scan, just to be sure. Even though I have no symptoms. No fever. No pain. Normal stools. I feel like I need a scan to know I'm safe."

Reassurance-seeking can momentarily calm fear, but it rarely teaches the mind that safety already exists.

Her husband, she said quietly, had called her selfish.

"He says I'm always thinking about my health and not about the kids or the family. But I can't help it. These thoughts don't stop. I try so hard, but I can't control them."

As she spoke, I could see the exhaustion of someone fighting her own mind every single day. Her guilt and her fear were so tightly woven that she could not separate one from the other.

"What you're experiencing," I said gently,
"is not selfishness. It's medical trauma."

She looked at me then, surprised. Relieved. Understood.

"When you were admitted," I continued,
"your brain went into survival mode. Every detail, the smells,

the sounds, the words, became linked to danger. Your body healed long ago, but your mind is still trying to protect you from a fear that no longer exists."

Her shoulders dropped slightly, as if releasing a burden she had been carrying alone for far too long.

"Your thoughts," I said softly,
"are not warnings. They are memories."

Her breath slowed. It was the first sign that her mind was beginning to understand she was not broken, only scared.

"I don't want to live like this," she whispered.
"I want peace."

And in that moment, the moment she allowed herself to name what she longed for, healing quietly began.

Health anxiety does not mean illness.
It means the mind is still protecting you from a past fear.

You are not weak.
You are not selfish.
You are not imagining your pain.

You are someone who experienced something frightening, and your mind is learning how to trust your body again.

With every steady breath,
every truth you write down,
every fear you choose to postpone,

you are teaching your brain something powerful:

I am safe now.
My body has healed.
My mind is learning to trust again.

And this is how peace returns. Slowly. Gently. One truth at a time.

Healing is not about never feeling fear.
Healing is when you can look at fear and say,

"Thank you for trying to protect me… but I am safe now."

Each time you remind your mind of this, you move one quiet inch closer to peace.

Many people live with health anxiety, It does not mean something is wrong with your body. It means your mind learned to stay alert during a frightening time and has not yet learned that safety has returned.

The practices that follow are not meant to eliminate fear, but to gently teach your nervous system how to tell the difference between memory and reality.

Take them slowly. You do not need to do everything.

HEALING PRACTICES

For Health Anxiety, Fear, and Medical Trauma

1. Separating Assumption from Fact

Health anxiety builds stories quickly. Healing begins when we slow those stories down.

When fear arises, gently separate assumption from fact.

An assumption might sound like:
Maybe the fluid has come back.
A fact sounds like:
I have no fever, no pain, normal stools, and no symptoms.

If it helps, write them side by side.
Something is wrong again — My tests were clear.
I need a scan to feel safe — Doctors did not advise further testing..

The brain calms when it is shown evidence, not reassurance alone.

2. Evidence Collection

Each time fear appears, write down a few simple things:

What fear is saying.
What your body is actually feeling.
Any real symptoms (if there are none, write "none").
What your doctor last said.
Why this fear might be repeating now.

Writing slows the spiral and brings the mind back to the present.

3. Postponing the Urge (The 20-Minute Rule)

When you feel the urge to search symptoms, ask for reassurance, book tests, or repeatedly check your body, pause.

Tell yourself:
I will wait for twenty minutes.

During that time, breathe slowly, walk a little, distract yourself gently, or write the fear down. Most urges lose their intensity when they are not immediately acted upon.

4. The Fear-or-Body Question

When panic rises, ask yourself one grounding question:

Is this fear, or is this a physical fact?

If there is no fever, no pain, no bleeding, no weakness, and no medical concern, then this is fear replaying a hospital memory, not a present danger.

5. Memory Trigger Awareness

When hospital images or medical thoughts return suddenly, remind yourself:

This is a memory, not a warning. My body is safe now.

This statement helps the mind place the fear in the past, where it belongs.

6. The Safety Check-In

Place your hand gently on your stomach or chest and ask:

Is there actual pain right now?
Is my breathing steady?
Is there any new symptom?

If the answer is no, say quietly:
My body is calm. Only my thoughts are loud.

7. Limiting Google Searches

Set a compassionate boundary with yourself.

Decide: *I do not Google symptoms.*
If fear persists for more than twenty-four hours or new symptoms appear, speak to a doctor, not the internet.

This protects your nervous system from unnecessary alarm.

8. The Calming Breath for Health Fear

When spiralling begins, use your breath to signal safety.

Inhale for four seconds.
Hold for two.
Exhale for six.

Repeat this five times, allowing your shoulders to soften as you breathe out.

9. Strengthening the Present Moment

Fear pulls the mind into "what if."

Gently bring yourself back by saying:
Right now, in this moment, I am safe.

Say it as many times as needed.

10. Rebuilding Trust in Your Body

Choose one or two simple daily habits that support your body.
Good sleep.
Walking.
Regular meals.
Hydration.
Sunlight.

These quiet acts send a powerful message to the mind:
My body is functioning well. I am safe.

Reflective Prompt:
Write down one health-related thought that scared you recently. Then gently separate assumption from fact.

*****

***"What you resist, persists."* — Carl Jung**
Fears increase when we try too hard to fight or avoid them; facing them gently reduces their power.

CHAPTER FIVE

You Are Not Too Much

After a long pause, she added,
"I feel like everyone else knows how to live… except me."

She was not asking for advice. She was asking for a place where she did not need to pretend, where she did not have to be strong, lovable, impressive, or healed.

She sat in the chair with a kind of exhaustion that had nothing to do with her body. It was the exhaustion of the heart, the kind that comes from being hurt, misunderstood, and disappointed one time too many.

"I'm back on medication," she said quietly.
"Depression. Relapse. Borderline personality disorder. I don't even feel shocked anymore."

Diagnoses can describe patterns of pain, but they do not describe the worth or depth of a person.

Her voice did not shake. That was the sign of how deep her tiredness ran. Pain that becomes familiar no longer feels dramatic; it simply becomes heavy.

She lived with her parents and brother, yet every sentence carried the loneliness of someone who had felt alone for most of her life.

"My marriage ended three years ago," she said.
"It was arranged. He tortured me mentally and physically. He didn't trust me. I think my depression started there."

During the first year of marriage, she lived abroad while he remained in India, separated by COVID and circumstance. When they finally lived together, things only worsened. Arguments replaced affection. Suspicion replaced trust.

"I went back abroad," she whispered.
"I couldn't stay."

Later, she returned to India, leaving behind her friends, her comfort, and the support system she had built for herself.

Now she was working on a new project, trying to learn everything at once.

"My days are just working and sleeping," she said.
"I have no space for myself."

Her body had begun speaking in ways her heart had not been able to.

Acid reflux.
Digestive issues.
Insomnia.
Persistent joint inflammation.

Small symptoms carried big fear. When the heart is tired, even a minor ache can feel like the beginning of a storm.

When emotional pain goes unheard for too long, the body often becomes the voice that speaks instead.

"I'm scared about my health," she admitted.
"Whenever I feel sick, I think I'll be alone. I think no one will be there."

It was not illness she feared. It was abandonment. For someone who has felt emotionally alone for years, illness can feel terrifying not because of pain, but because of the fear of having no one to turn to.

"I'm in my early thirties. Still single," she said softly.
"Maybe my standards are high. Maybe nobody wants a woman like me."

Her voice cracked, not loudly, but like a quiet breaking somewhere deep inside.

Occasional age-related remarks from colleagues made her uncomfortable. One day, she finally spoke back, not because she was angry, but because she was exhausted from being belittled.

"I feel judged everywhere," she whispered.
"At home. At work. In relationships. There's no place where I feel understood."

She had come to counselling because she had realised something important.

"Medicines can help my brain," she said slowly.
"But counselling… maybe it can help my heart."

She was not wrong.

Then came the truth she had been carrying since childhood.

"My parents were never emotionally supportive," she said. "They judged me, dismissed me, never really understood my feelings. I think I've been longing for love ever since I was a little girl."

That little girl had grown into a woman still searching for the warmth she never received.

"And men…" she sighed.
"Every man I trusted hurt me. Boyfriends. My husband. Almost every connection. Betrayal. Manipulation. Insecurity. Lies."

She paused, her voice dropping to a whisper.

"I'm scared to trust again. But I'm also scared of being alone forever. When I get sick… I'm scared I'll die alone."

In that one sentence lived all her wounds.

Exhaustion.
Abandonment.
Loneliness.
Longing for love.
Fear of repeating the past.

I leaned toward her gently.

"You are not too much," I said softly.
"You have simply been loved too little."

A tear finally escaped, the kind that comes when someone speaks the words you have needed to hear your entire life.

"You don't need the perfect man," I continued.
"You need someone safe. But before that… you need safety within yourself."

Seeking connection is not weakness. It becomes painful only when it is the sole source of safety.

She took a slow breath.

"You keep asking, 'Will someone love me?'" I said gently.
"But the deeper question is, 'Do I love myself enough to not collapse without someone?'"

Her eyes softened. She understood.

Love from others is meant to be a blessing, not survival.
What she needed was partnership, not rescue.

"You want love," I said,
"not because you are empty, but because you are ready."

She nodded. Exhausted. Hurting. But now, quietly hopeful.

That is where healing begins.

The longing to be loved is one of the most human desires. Yet when self-worth has been wounded, love can feel distant or unsafe. Her story reminds us that doubt in our value is not truth, but a scar carried from past experiences. Healing begins when we stop measuring our worth by other's acceptance and start recognising the quiet strength that has always been within us.

The practices that follow are invitations to reconnect with that strength and allow love to feel safe again. Move through them gently. This is not a checklist to complete, but a relationship to build with yourself.

HEALING PRACTICES

For Those Who Feel Unseen, Unloved, and Afraid of Being Alone

1. The Emotional Safety Check

Before seeking connection, pause and ask yourself:

Do I feel emotionally safe with myself right now?

If the answer is no, it may be a sign to slow down, not to punish yourself, but to restore your own sense of grounding first. Emotional safety within often shapes the safety we experience with others.

2. The "I Matter" Daily Practice

Once a day, spend a few quiet minutes writing:

Three things you did well today.
One thing you handled better than last time.
One strength you often forget you have.

This practice slowly retrains the mind to recognise worth that is not dependent on others' approval.

3. The Slow Love Rule

If a connection feels rushed, overwhelming, or intensely emotional very early, pause.

Love that heals does not demand urgency.
It grows warm, steady, consistent, and deep over time.

When attachment forms too quickly, it is often driven by fear of loss rather than genuine safety.

4. The Boundary Sentence

When something feels uncomfortable or emotionally unsafe, quietly name it to yourself:

This doesn't feel emotionally safe for me.

You do not always need to explain or justify this feeling. Awareness itself is a form of protection.

5. The Red-Flag Reset

If someone consistently makes you anxious, confused, disrespected, pressured, or unseen, pause.

Your task is not to work harder for approval.
Your task is to step back and notice what your body and emotions are telling you.

Walking away from what harms you is an act of self-respect.

6. Love Readiness, Not Perfection

You are not required to be fully healed to be loved. Readiness simply means you can choose without fear driving every decision.

You may be ready when you no longer settle out of loneliness, when you choose slowly instead of urgently, when you recognise your worth, when you can set boundaries, and when you can be alone without collapsing.

This is not a test. It is a direction.

7. The Self-Compassion Breath

When emotions feel overwhelming, place one hand on your chest.

As you inhale, say silently: *I am here for me.*
As you exhale, say: *This moment will pass.*

Repeat this five times, allowing your breath to soften.

8. Observing Yourself with Kindness

When you feel triggered, jealous, abandoned, or insecure, pause and ask:

What is this feeling trying to tell me?

Curiosity opens space. Judgment closes it.

9. Creating a Life Beyond One Relationship

Love grows best when it is part of a full life, not the only source of meaning.

Write down two or three areas that deserve your energy right now.
Your work. Your interests. Your friendships. Your health. Your learning. Your spiritual or inner life.

These anchors make connection safer, not colder.

10. The Emotional Independence Builder

Before turning to someone else for reassurance, try offering support to yourself.

Breathe slowly.
Write a few lines.
Take a walk.
Hold yourself gently.
Drink something warm.
Speak to yourself with kindness.
Engage in something that interests you.

Self-support does not replace love. It strengthens your capacity to receive it.

Reflective Prompt:
Ask yourself: "If I were my own partner, how would I show love to me today?"

*****

***"People are just as wonderful as sunsets if you let them be."* — Carl Rogers**

We heal when we stop forcing ourselves to be perfect and allow space for natural growth and acceptance.

CHAPTER SIX

Love Without Losing Yourself

For a moment, he remained standing near the door, as if deciding whether he had the strength to speak the truth today.

When he finally sat down, his shoulders dropped. It was the posture of someone who had been holding tension for far too long.

He did not begin with explanations or rush into details. His fingers were tightly interlocked, his gaze fixed on the space between his shoes, as though that small patch of floor felt safer than looking at the life he was about to describe.

There was no anger in his silence. No bitterness. Only a quiet, heavy fear, the kind that forms when someone has been trying to hold a family together long after their strength has begun to run out.

When he finally spoke, the words came carefully, like something he had rehearsed alone for months.

"Madam… my house doesn't feel like a home anymore," he said quietly.

"My marriage is ten years old. And for the first time… I am scared of the home I built."

He was not dramatic. He was not blaming. He was a man caught between love, duty, and survival, each pulling him in a different direction, leaving him unsure where to stand.

He and his wife had three children. Their marriage had been arranged. Only after the wedding did he learn the parts no one had spoken about before.

His wife had no formal education.
Her family carried a history of psychological struggles.
One of her siblings had died by suicide.

And yet, he stayed.

Staying was not denial. It was responsibility, hope, and a deep desire to protect his children and the life he had promised to hold together.

He adjusted. He built a life around the truth he had discovered.

For years, he managed the home. He worked hard. He cared for the children. He tried to be patient with everything his wife struggled with.

But something had changed recently, something beyond his understanding.

"My wife has become very paranoid," he said softly.
"She suspects me of affairs with anyone I speak to… even my aunt."

He swallowed the next truth, as though it burned on the way up.

"She makes these accusations publicly. She sent messages blaming me and threatening self-harm in our community group, saying I'm responsible."

He paused, his jaw tightening. A man holding back a storm.

"I think she's emotionally blackmailing me," he whispered. "I don't know how to live like this anymore."

But the deepest wound had not yet been spoken.

She had made serious accusations that disturbed him deeply and affected his relationship with his children. He was not crying, but the pain in his eyes was unmistakable, the kind only a father carries.

"I tried family counselling," he said.
"She refused. She won't cooperate with anything. I live under constant stress. I have headaches every day."

For safety and emotional stability, the children were now staying with his parents. Protecting children from emotional volatility is not rejection of a parent, but protection of a developing nervous system.

"I don't know how to handle all this," he murmured.
"I'm scared for them. And I'm scared for myself."

He was not a man trying to abandon his family. He was a man trying not to lose himself inside a crisis that had grown too heavy for one person to carry alone.

I leaned gently into the stillness between us.

"You are doing more than any one person can do by themselves," I said softly.
"And it is okay to say… this is too much."

His eyes softened. Relief and grief mingled together. For the first time in years, someone had told him he did not need to be superhuman.

Life sometimes pushes us into roles we never expected to play. We become caretakers, crisis managers, emotional buffers, protectors, the strong one, the one who absorbs everything.

And somewhere along the way, we forget that we are human too.

When a partner lives with paranoia, emotional instability, severe insecurity, unresolved trauma, or untreated psychological conditions, their inner chaos often spills into the home. It reaches the children. It reaches the partner. Not because they want to hurt anyone, but because their inner world feels unsafe. This does not mean harm is acceptable, but it helps us understand that pain is often acted out before it is understood.

Slowly, the caregiving partner begins to break.

We forget something essential.

Supporting someone does not mean sacrificing our sanity.
Loving someone does not mean tolerating chaos.
Commitment does not mean staying silent while being destroyed.

Healing begins with honesty.

You cannot fix another person's mind by breaking your own.
You cannot save someone alone.
You cannot raise children inside fear.

Love should not feel like walking on broken glass every day. Boundaries are not an exit from love; they are often the only way love survives without destroying the people inside it. Boundaries, clarity, and safety are not abandonment. They are acts of love.

We do not fail when relationships become difficult. We fail only when we abandon ourselves completely.

Protecting our mind, our children, our peace, and our emotional truth is not selfishness. It is the foundation of healthy love.

Sometimes, the strongest thing we can say is:

"I will stand with you, but I will not lose myself in the process."

That strength is what keeps families safe.

Responsibility can sometimes press down on love until joy quietly disappears. His story reminds us that fear often grows when duty overshadows tenderness, leaving the heart exhausted and unsure of its place. Living with someone whose emotions feel unpredictable can quietly exhaust the nervous system. Healing begins when responsibility is carried with balance when we honour our limits, protect emotional space, and allow love to feel safe again.

The practices given below are not about giving up on love. They are about protecting safety, dignity, and emotional balance, especially when caregiving begins to consume everything.

Move through these gently. You are not expected to do everything at once.

HEALING PRACTICES

For Anyone Living With a Partner Whose Emotions, Accusations, or Instability Feel Overwhelming

1. Protecting Emotional Space

When someone is overwhelmed by paranoia or emotional instability, reasoning in the moment often escalates distress.

In those moments, the first step is safety.
Stay calm.
Avoid arguing or explaining.
Create emotional distance when needed.

This is not punishment. It is protection.

2. Care Without Carrying Everything Alone

Remind yourself gently:

Their struggle is real.
I am not the cause.
I cannot be the cure on my own.

Care becomes harmful when it demands self-erasure.

3. Prioritising Children's Safety

When children are involved, ask yourself quietly:

Where will they feel safest right now?
Who can provide consistent, calm care?
How can we reduce their exposure to fear or conflict?

Protecting children from emotional volatility is an act of love, not rejection.

4. Boundaries Without Aggression

Boundaries do not need to be loud to be firm.

You might say:
I don't want to discuss this when emotions are high.
Let's talk later when we're both calmer.
I won't argue, but I'm here when things settle.

Clarity is kinder than silence.

5. Releasing Accusations as Truth

When accusations arise, remind yourself:

These words come from fear, not from my reality.

You are not required to absorb another person's distress as evidence against yourself.

6. Building a Support Circle

Support may come from parents, siblings, close friends, counsellors, or trusted community members.

You do not have to carry this alone. Isolation makes everything heavier.

7. Creating a Calm Routine

Simple daily grounding practices help restore balance.

Slow breathing.
Short walks.
Warm baths.
Journaling.
Soft music.
Quiet pauses.

Consistency matters more than intensity.

8. Quiet Documentation

Without confrontation or blame, keep a private record of significant concerns, threats, extreme accusations, public posts, or refusals of counselling.

This is not about punishment. It is about clarity and safety, especially when decisions must be made later.

9. Pausing Before Responding

When emotions rise, practice a pause.

Pause.
Breathe.
Observe.
Respond later.

Delayed responses are often the wisest ones.

10. Gentle Long-Term Planning

Ask yourself, without panic:

If this continues, what support will my children need?
What support do I need?
Who else can be involved?
What boundaries protect dignity and safety?

Planning is not betrayal. It is responsibility.

11. Accepting Truth With Compassion

Tell yourself:

My partner is not choosing to be unwell.
But I cannot lose myself while trying to help.

Both truths can exist together

12. Supporting Without Saving

Shift the inner narrative from:

I must fix everything
to
I will support what is healthy and protect what is unsafe.

This shift protects love from becoming self-destruction.

Reflective Prompt:
Pause and ask: "Where do I need boundaries right now to protect my peace?"

*****

***"People will do anything, no matter how absurd, to avoid facing their own souls."* — Carl Jung**
Unprocessed pain often turns into blame, suspicion, or chaos directed outward.

CHAPTER SEVEN

Choosing Peace Over Pressure

She walked in with a smile that did not quite reach her eyes, the kind people wear when they are trying to appear fine for the world while quietly falling apart inside.

She placed her phone on the table gently, almost ceremonially, as if the device itself carried too many opinions, too many expectations, too many voices pulling her in opposite directions.

This was not confusion about her boyfriend or her family alone. It was confusion about herself, about the part of her heart that loved deeply, and the part that feared hurting the people who had raised her.

"We've known each other for three years," she began softly. "Two years in a relationship. We met in Bangalore when I worked in the private sector. Then I got my government job and moved to a different city."

Warmth entered her voice when she spoke about him.

"He supported me through everything. I got emotionally attached. He is understanding, kind, steady."

But the moment she began speaking about her family, something inside her tightened.

"We told our families. Mine didn't take it well. They feel I betrayed them… because he comes from a different background."

She paused, swallowing guilt that did not truly belong to her.

"I come from a joint family. We live closely. My brother and sister-in-law say they support my happiness, but they also say he may not be suitable."

It was never just one reason.

It was caste.
It was height.
It was appearance.
It was tradition.
It was society.
It was fear disguised as concern.

"My parents keep saying, 'We gave you everything. We supported you. We let you study, work in another city, live independently. How could you betray us like this?'"

Her eyes softened with pain.

"And the thing is… they did support me," she said quietly. "Especially when I met with a major accident and needed a long recovery. They stood by me."

Gratitude creates connection, not lifelong surrender of one's future.

She looked down then, her voice lowering.

"But he stood by me too. Every single day. He never once made me feel like a burden. Even his family was understanding about my limitations. They didn't judge me for being physically weak."

This was not a story of choosing between two people. It was a story of choosing between two forms of love.

Choosing one form of love does not automatically cancel the other, even when fear makes it feel that way.

"We had decided earlier," she said,
"that we would proceed with marriage only if both families accepted. Otherwise, we would end it."

Her voice trembled.

"But now I don't know what to do. I'm confused how to choose. Love marriage or arranged marriage? My family or my partner? My happiness or their expectations?"

I could feel her heart stretched between gratitude and desire, between tradition and individuality, between old love and new love.

"You are not choosing between right and wrong," I said gently.
"You are choosing between two things that matter in different ways."

She exhaled slowly, a release she did not know she had been holding.

When we grow up in families that love deeply and sacrifice silently, we carry invisible responsibilities. The responsibility not to hurt them. Not to disappoint them. Not to break their dreams for us. Not to appear ungrateful.

So when love enters our life from a direction they did not expect, the conflict becomes more than marriage. It becomes a struggle between loyalty and identity, guilt and desire, tradition and autonomy, fear and freedom. Pressure often speaks louder than truth, but it does not make it wiser.

But emotional truth is often simple.

We are allowed to love our family.
We are allowed to love our partner.
We are allowed to honour our parents.
We are allowed to honour our future.
We are allowed to feel grateful and still choose what gives us emotional peace.

Choosing peace is not selfishness; it is responsibility toward the life you must live every day.

We do not lose our family by choosing ourselves. We lose ourselves by trying to please everyone.

We do not betray our family by choosing a partner. We betray ourselves when we abandon our truth.

Life becomes gentler when we understand this:

Love is not a choice between two people. It is a choice between fear and truth.

And when decisions come from clarity rather than pressure, from inner calm rather than guilt, we build a future we can stand beside without regret.

Family expectations can stretch the heart in opposite directions, pulling between love and duty until it slowly frays. Her story reminds us that the burden of pleasing others can silence our own truth, making us feel as though choosing love is betrayal or choosing family is rejection. Yet authenticity is never betrayal. It is the beginning of peace.

Healing begins when we pause, breathe, clarify our values, and gently separate truth from pressure. The practices that follow are designed to help you slow down, create space for your own voice, soften the weight of expectation, and move toward choices that feel genuine, grounded, and aligned with your long-term well-being.

You are allowed to take time. Clarity grows gently.

HEALING PRACTICES

For Anyone Caught Between Love, Family Expectations, Guilt, and Confusion

1. Clarifying Emotional Needs

Begin by asking yourself what you truly need to feel emotionally safe in marriage.

You might need respect, support, trust, kindness, stability, or emotional understanding. Notice which of these your current partner offers, and which feel non-negotiable for your future.

This is not about judging anyone. It is about listening to yourself.

2. Identifying Core Values

Write down the values that matter most to you. These may include family bonds, independence, equality, emotional connection, cultural continuity, or long-term stability.

Then reflect quietly.
Which values feel essential to who you are?
Which align with your partner?
Which feel pressured rather than chosen within your family expectations?

Values clarify what fear often confuses.

3. Visualising the Life Ahead

Without rushing, imagine your future in two different paths.

With your partner, ask yourself:
Does the relationship feel emotionally safe?
Can we face challenges together?
Is there room for growth, adjustment, and mutual respect?

With an arranged match, ask:
Will I feel respected and understood?
Will I be able to be myself?
Will I feel supported during vulnerability?

Notice not which future looks perfect, but which one feels more peaceful in your body.

4. Separating Truth from Pressure

Ask yourself gently:

If no one were influencing me, what would I choose?
If I chose differently, what are the actual consequences, not the imagined ones?

Pressure speaks loudly. Truth speaks quietly.

5. Checking the Relationship Honestly

Look at the relationship itself, not just the story around it.

Is there trust?
Open communication?
Emotional consistency?
Support during difficult times?
A willingness to resolve conflict with care?

Love that lasts feels steady, not consuming.

6. Remembering That Fear Creates Regret

When anxiety rises, remind yourself:

I do not need to decide today.
I am allowed time.
I am allowed clarity.

Decisions made in fear often leave regret. Decisions made in calm create peace.

7. Acknowledging Family Feelings Without Losing Yourself

It is possible to validate family emotions without abandoning your own.

You may say:
I understand your fear.
I know this is difficult for you.
I value everything you have done for me.

And still remain honest about your desires.

Empathy does not require self-betrayal.

8. Preparing for Family Conversations

Before speaking with family, write down what truly matters to you.

When you speak, keep your tone calm and grounded. You might say:
I need time to think. I want to make a decision that brings clarity and peace.

You are allowed to ask for space without guilt.

9. Releasing the Belief That Happiness Is Betrayal

Repeat gently, as often as needed:

I can honour my parents and make my own choices.
Both can coexist.

Your happiness does not erase their love.

10. Choosing Long-Term Peace Over Short-Term Approval

Finally, ask yourself one honest question:

Which choice will allow me to breathe freely five years from now?

That answer is not impulsive.
It is your truth, waiting patiently to be heard.

Reflective Prompt:

Imagine yourself five years ahead. Which choice today would allow you to breathe freely then?

*****

"When I look at the world I am pessimistic, but when I look at people I am optimistic."

— Carl Rogers

Human beings often show more kindness and understanding than the systems and pressures around them.

CHAPTER EIGHT

From Hiding To healing

His steps were small and measured, the way people walk when they have spent years trying not to be noticed.

He did not speak like someone telling a story. He spoke like a man finally allowing his childhood to breathe after decades of suffocation.

"In my early childhood," he began, "an elder molested me."

He did not pause for effect. He paused because the sentence still hurt.

"He was punished publicly," he continued.
"But after that… everyone looked at me."

Not at the abuser.
Not at the crime.
At him.

In a small community, the incident became public shame. It was exposure. It was humiliation wrapped in the disguise of justice.

"Kids bullied me," he whispered.
"They teased me. Made fun of me. I felt like I had done something wrong."

He was a child carrying an adult's shame, a shame that never belonged to him.

"I think that's when everything changed," he said softly.
"I stopped feeling normal. I stopped feeling safe."

Trauma does not only wound. It rewires. It teaches the body to survive instead of to live. When trauma happens in childhood, the body carries it forward until it is finally understood, not until time passes.

As he grew older, the wound grew with him, silently and invisibly.

"I get anxious in social situations," he said.
"My body starts sweating. My mind freezes. In presentations, meetings, family functions… I just can't speak."

He was not afraid of people. He was afraid of being seen. The first time he was truly seen, he was humiliated.

"I avoid gatherings," he added.
"I avoid presentations. I avoid anything where people might look at me."

His voice cracked, not loudly, but in a way that revealed a lifetime of withdrawal.

"I compare myself with everyone," he said.
"They're getting promotions, recognition, a good life. I know I'm academically better than many. But because of this anxiety, I miss opportunities. I stay small. I feel like I'm losing everywhere."

This was not laziness.
It was paralysis.

This was not lack of talent.
It was unhealed trauma.

This was not lack of confidence.
It was a childhood fear that the world would shame him again.

"I don't feel unconditional love," he said quietly.
"I don't feel genuinely happy."

He was not broken. He was exhausted from hiding, from pretending, from fighting memories alone.

I leaned in gently.

"You learned to hide because the world made your pain visible," I said softly.
"And your body is still protecting you from being seen."

He looked at me in stunned silence, the kind that comes when someone hears their truth for the first time.

"You did not lose confidence," I continued.
"It was taken from you at an age when your mind could not understand what was happening."

His breath trembled, relief wrapped in grief.

"Your social anxiety," I said gently,
"is not your flaw. It is your body's way of saying, I do not want to be seen the way I was seen when I was at my weakest."

For the first time, tears formed, not from weakness, but from recognition. The child inside him had waited decades to be understood.

A small boy learned to hide because the world exposed his pain. But the man sitting here today is not that helpless child. He is a survivor. Intelligent. Capable. Sensitive. Strong.

He did not lose his future. He only paused it. And now, slowly, gently, bravely, he is learning to be seen again.

Healing will not take him back to who he once was. It will take him forward into who he was always meant to become.

Not every quiet child grows up without wounds. Some learn early that disappearing keeps them safe. His story shows how deeply these lessons settle into the body, shaping what we later call social anxiety. What began as protection in childhood can become invisibility in adulthood, and shrinking ourselves is never weakness. It is survival.

Healing begins when we gently teach the body that visibility is no longer dangerous. The practices that follow are designed to support anyone healing from childhood trauma, shame, or social anxiety to rebuild trust in connection, soften the fear of judgment, and step into visibility with safety, dignity, and self-worth. Move slowly. Healing unfolds at its own pace.

HEALING PRACTICES

For Anyone Healing From Childhood Trauma, Shame, or Social Anxiety

1. Separating Yourself From Trauma

Begin by reminding yourself:

This response belongs to trauma, not to who I am.

Fear learned in childhood can linger into adulthood, even when danger is no longer present. Naming this separation restores dignity.

2. Relearning Social Safety in Small Steps

Social confidence is rebuilt gradually, not all at once.

You might begin by speaking a single sentence in a meeting. On another day, you might attend a gathering briefly. Later, you may try presenting for a short time or joining a group conversation.

There is no fixed order. Expand only when your body feels ready.

3. Using Somatic Grounding

When anxiety rises, return to the body.

Press your feet firmly into the ground.
Hold a cold object.
Lengthen your exhale.
Name five objects you can see.
Relax your jaw and shoulders.

The body calms before the mind follows.

4. Challenging the Fear of Judgment

When fear speaks, ask gently:

Where is the evidence right now?
Is this fear from the past, or the present moment?

You are allowed to question fear without fighting it.

5. Releasing Comparison

When comparison appears, remind yourself:

They did not carry my trauma.
I am not behind.
I am healing.

Healing follows its own timeline.

6. Rebuilding Self-Worth Through Micro-Confidence

Confidence grows through small, repeated experiences.

You might share one opinion, make one decision, practice a short response, express a need, or take on a small responsibility.

Each action teaches your nervous system that expression is safe.

7. Re-Parenting the Wounded Child

Speak gently to the younger part of you:

You were innocent.
You did not deserve shame.
You deserved protection.

This is not imagination. It is emotional repair.

8. Rewriting Identity Through Ability

Begin anchoring your identity in what is real today:

I am intelligent.
I am capable.
I am growing.
I am healing.

Identity strengthens through repetition, not force.

9. Creating a Recognition Plan

Recognition does not come from sudden visibility. It grows with preparation and support.

You might volunteer for small tasks, practice with a trusted person, take limited presentation roles, prepare thoroughly, and acknowledge every attempt.

Progress counts, even when it feels quiet.

10. Remembering What Healing Truly Is

Healing does not mean becoming fearless.

Remind yourself:

Visibility is not danger.
My voice is allowed.
My presence is valid.

Freedom comes not from erasing fear, but from no longer letting fear decide who you are allowed to be.

Reflective Prompt:
Think of one situation where you hid yourself recently. What small step could you take to be seen safely next time?

*****

"I am not what others have done to me." **— Carl Jung**
Experiences shape us, but they do not define our worth or limit our future potential.

CHAPTER NINE

Exhaustion Is Not Hopelessness

He sat down slowly, almost sinking into the chair, as if the weight he carried had followed him all the way into the room.

For a moment, he did not speak. He stared at his palms, as though searching for a version of himself he once knew.

"Madam… I don't know what I'm doing with my life," he said finally.

He did not say he was sad. He did not say he was depressed. He simply said,
"I feel low. Lost. No energy."

Sometimes the deepest pain hides behind the simplest words.

"I have one younger sister," he began.
"And one half-sibling. I lost my mother when I was fourteen."

He said it like a fact, but it was not just a fact. It was a turning point his life never truly recovered from.

"When my father remarried, everything changed," he said quietly.

"I lost the image of my father. And my stepmother was abusive."

There was no anger in his voice. Only fatigue. The exhaustion of someone who spent his childhood surviving instead of living.

"I struggled a lot," he whispered.
"But I completed my studies. Somehow."

That single word carried years of silent battles.

During his undergraduate years, he fell in love.

"But we broke up," he said.
"And it broke something in me."

He did not dramatise it. He did not blame her. He simply acknowledged a loss that added itself to the many losses he already carried.

Later, he went abroad for his post-graduation. People often imagine that moving to another country heals emotional pain. But pain travels. It does not need a passport.

"I came back," he said softly.
"I'm working now, but I feel hopeless. I don't know what I'm doing with my life."

He was not lost because he lacked direction. He was lost because he never had emotional ground to stand on.

When loss happens early and repeatedly, the nervous system grows tired before the person ever has a chance to grow steady.

Then he said the words many people hide.

"I'm having addiction problems," he admitted.
"Smoking. Drinking. I think I'm using them to escape."

He did not need me to confirm it. He already knew.

He was not weak. He was tired.
He was not irresponsible. He was hurting.

Sometimes addiction is not about pleasure. It is about numbness. A temporary escape from a life that has felt too heavy for too long.

As he spoke, a pattern became clear.

A boy lost his mother.
A teenager lost his father emotionally.
A young man lost his first love.
And the adult he became slowly lost himself.

I leaned in gently.

"You have been surviving for so long," I said softly,
"that you have forgotten what living feels like."

His eyes softened, finally feeling recognised.

"You did not grow up with safety," I continued.
"You grew up learning to hold your emotions alone. Now your mind is tired. Your body is tired. Your heart is tired."

Sometimes clarity is not complicated. It is compassionate.

"You are not hopeless," I said quietly.
"You are exhausted. There is a difference."

Exhaustion often wears the mask of hopelessness. When the body is depleted and the mind is heavy, hope can feel distant. His story reminds us that weariness is not failure. It is a call for rest.

When life has asked too much for too long, the body slows down, the mind grows heavy, and motivation disappears. This does not mean you are failing. It means you are tired.

The practices below are not meant to fix you. They are meant to help you rest, understand yourself, and take small steps toward steadiness again. Move gently. Healing does not require urgency.

HEALING PRACTICES

For Anyone Who Feels Lost, Low, Overwhelmed, or Stuck in Addiction or Emotional Exhaustion

1. Validating Exhaustion

Feeling low is not a sign of weakness. It is a sign that your mind and body have been carrying more than they could comfortably hold.

Remind yourself:
I am tired because my life has been demanding, not because I have failed.

2. Acknowledging Your Emotional Story

Give yourself quiet space to reflect.

What have you been carrying alone?
Which painful memories still live inside you?
Where do you feel unseen or unsupported?
What parts of your life have felt especially heavy?

Naming the story reduces its weight.

3. Releasing Comparison With Others

When comparison arises, ask yourself gently:

Did they live my life?
Did they face my pain?

You are not behind. You are healing from experiences others never had to survive.

4. Listening to What Emptiness Is Saying

Instead of fighting emptiness, become curious about it.

Are you emotionally drained?
Longing for connection?
Overwhelmed by decisions?
Ignoring your own needs?

Emptiness is often a message, not a flaw.

5. Looking at Coping Habits With Compassion

Behaviours like smoking, drinking, or endless scrolling are often attempts to escape pain, not signs of irresponsibility.

Ask yourself gently:
What am I trying to numb?
What pain am I avoiding?
What emotion usually comes before the urge?

Understanding comes before change.

6. Creating Simple Grounding Rituals

When everything feels too much, return to small anchors.

Slow breathing.
Splashing cold water on your face.
Walking for five minutes.
Listening to calming music.
Stretching briefly.
Writing one honest sentence about how you feel.

Small rituals steady the nervous system.

7. Rebuilding Daily Structure Gently

Structure restores safety, but it must be kind.

You might aim to wake up at a similar time, eat one nourishing meal, complete one simple task, step outside for fresh air, or slightly reduce one addictive behaviour.

Consistency matters more than perfection.

8. Reconnecting With Your Strengths

Write down what reminds you of who you are beneath exhaustion.

What are you naturally good at?
What has life already taught you?
How have you survived difficult times before?

Strength does not disappear. It gets buried under fatigue.

9. Reducing Loneliness Through One Safe Connection

Healing does not require many people. It begins with one.

A trusted friend.
A sibling.
A therapist.
A mentor.
A supportive colleague.

One steady connection can soften a lot of pain.

10. Practicing Emotional Honesty

Instead of saying "I'm fine," try telling the truth in simple ways.

I feel overwhelmed.
I feel disconnected.
I need support.

Honesty creates relief.

11. Offering Yourself Daily Permission

Repeat gently, especially on hard days:

I am allowed to heal slowly.
I am allowed to rebuild my life.
I am allowed to feel lost and still move forward.

Progress does not always feel like movement. Sometimes it feels like rest.

Reflective Prompt:
Think of one coping habit you use when life feels heavy. What emotion is it trying to soothe?

*****

"The most basic of all human needs is to be understood." **— Carl Rogers**

Many emotional struggles soften when a person finally feels heard and validated.

CHAPTER TEN

Fear Is Grief in Disguise

He did not sit like someone seeking answers. He sat like someone carrying too many questions in his chest, questions he had never had the courage or the words to express.

"I lost a young sibling during a global crisis," he said quietly. "She was very young, and it shattered me."

His voice did not break, but something deeper inside him did.

"I was abroad when she passed away," he continued.
"I could not process it. I had panic attacks. I admitted myself to the hospital three times."

He was not trying to be dramatic. He was trying to survive.

"I thought things would settle with time," he said softly.
"But recently, my father died of a heart attack."

There was no anger and no tears, only a tired fear. It was the kind of fear that forms when life keeps proving that everything can change in a single moment.

"All these things make me very fearful," he whispered.
"I feel like anything can happen at any time."

Even as he spoke, I could sense that his body was still living in the shock of those losses.

"Even when I was travelling back to India, sitting on the flight, I almost had a panic attack," he said.
"I did not know what I was scared of. But something inside me kept saying that something bad was going to happen."

It was not the flight or the height. It was the unpredictability of life. It was the fear of sudden loss and the memory of receiving devastating news from far away.

"Not only flight travel," he added.
"Even small things make me fearful. My mind jumps to the worst possibility."

"I feel like I could not overcome grief," he said quietly.
"I fear something will happen to my loved ones, or to me."

"But the way I feel, my emotions and my fears, I cannot make others understand," he continued.
"Even my own family sees me differently."

"When I try to explain, they look at me strangely, as if I am exaggerating, as if I am being too sensitive."

He was not overly emotional. He was grieving. He was anxious. He was living with emotional shock. But the world around him did not see that.

"I know it is hard for them," he said.
"They have not felt what I felt. But that makes me feel even more alone."

His loneliness was not from the absence of people. It came from being surrounded by people who could not understand the depth of his inner storm.

"I am better than before," he added.
"I did yoga. I saw a life coach. I am trying everything. But still, some part of me feels like I might have another episode. I want a permanent solution."

What he wanted was simple. Peace. Predictability. A mind that does not live in fear. A heart that feels safe again.

When someone dies unexpectedly, especially a sibling and especially at a young age, grief becomes intertwined with fear.

When loss arrives without warning, the nervous system does not measure time; it measures safety.

The mind learns a painful rule.
Bad things happen suddenly. Life can break without warning.

So the body becomes hyper-aware.
The heart becomes guarded.
Sleep becomes fragile.
Panic becomes familiar.

Small triggers become big reactions.
Travel feels unsafe.
Normal routines feel dangerous.

Nothing is actually wrong, but everything feels wrong.

This is not a character flaw.
This is not being too sensitive.
This is how trauma shapes the nervous system.

Fear becomes a language.
The body becomes the storyteller.
Every small moment feels like a possible threat.

And when family does not understand, grief becomes heavier and fear becomes lonelier.

But this matters.

You are not overreacting.
You are not weak.
You are not imagining things.

Your mind is still trying to protect you from a world that has hurt you in unexpected ways.

Your fear is not madness. It is grief that has not yet felt safe enough to heal.

He believed something was wrong with him, but nothing was wrong. He was grieving. He was scared. He was exhausted from losing too much, too soon. He was tired of being misunderstood. He was longing for safety.

And slowly, through awareness, grounding, consistency, and compassion, that sense of safety will return.

Grief does not disappear.
But fear loosens.
Panic softens.
The body relearns calm.
The heart relearns trust.

Life becomes steady again.
Not suddenly.
But slowly, gently, and deeply.

His story reminds us that grief often disguises itself as fear. When loss is sudden, the mind learns to expect danger everywhere, and the body carries that fear long after the moment has passed. Healing begins when we teach the nervous system that the danger is over, when we allow grief to exist without shame, and when we rebuild safety through gentle routines and compassionate connection. The practices that follow are designed for anyone grieving sudden loss and living with fear-driven anxiety.

Move gently. Healing does not require force.

HEALING PRACTICES

For Anyone Grieving Sudden Loss and Living With Fear-Driven Anxiety

When loss arrives without warning, the nervous system stays alert long after the danger has passed. Fear becomes the body's way of trying to prevent another heartbreak. These practices are not meant to erase grief, but to help your body slowly relearn safety while allowing sorrow to exist without shame.

1. Teaching the Body a Sense of Safety

Your body needs repeated signals that the present moment is calm.

You might offer this through slow breathing, warm showers, morning sunlight, or gentle grounding touch such as placing a hand on your chest.

Safety is learned through consistency, not logic.

2. Separating Trauma Memory From Present Danger

When fear rises, ask yourself quietly:

Is this happening right now?
Or is my mind reliving the fear of losing someone?

Naming the difference helps the nervous system settle.

3. Anchoring During Panic

If panic begins, focus on one step at a time.

First, name it gently: *This is panic, not danger.*
Then ground the body by pressing your feet into the floor, holding something cold, or lengthening your exhale.
Finally, orient to the present by looking around and naming five things you can see.

You do not need to rush. Panic passes when the body feels supported.

4. Allowing Grief to Exist

Grief does not need fixing. It needs space.

You may honour it through memories, photographs, tears, writing letters to your loved one, or speaking about them aloud.

Remembering is not regression. It is love.

5. Rebuilding Routine for Safety

Predictability helps calm fear.

Choose gentle anchors such as waking at a similar time, light movement or yoga, a simple morning ritual, consistent meals, or a quiet wind-down before sleep.

Routine reassures the body that life is steady again.

6. Softening Catastrophic Thinking

When fear spirals, write gently:

What triggered the fear?
What is the fear saying?
What are the facts right now?
What is one calming truth I can offer myself?

Facts ground what fear exaggerates.

7. Understanding Travel-Related Fear

If fear arises during travel, remind yourself:

This is a memory from the past, not danger in the present.

Use breath and grounding before and during travel to support your body.

8. Sharing With One Safe Person

You do not need to explain everything. One safe connection is enough.

A friend.
A sibling.
A therapist.
A partner.

You might simply say:
I am scared.
I am overwhelmed.
I am missing them.

Being heard reduces loneliness.

9. Bringing Compassion Into Healing

Notice when self-judgment appears.

Instead of asking, *Why am I still anxious?* or *Why can't I move on?*
Try telling yourself:
I am healing at my own pace.
This fear came from pain, not weakness.
I am slowly getting stronger.

Compassion accelerates healing more than criticism ever could.

10. Reminding Yourself That Peace Is Returning

Repeat gently, especially during fearful moments:

My mind is healing.
My fear is softening.
I am safe in this moment.
I will not always feel like this.

Peace often arrives quietly, before we even notice.

Reflective Prompt:
Think of one fear that feels overwhelming today. What gentle truth could soften it?

*****

"Mourning is the price we pay for loving." **— Sigmund Freud**
Deep grief reflects deep love; it is a natural and meaningful part of being human.

CHAPTER ELEVEN

Confusion Is Exhaustion in Disguise

A young woman with a slim frame and soft curls falling over her shoulders walked in, the kind of appearance people often assume signals calm, even when the heart is anything but calm.

She did not begin by talking about her stress. She began by describing her mornings.

"I wake up tired," she said.
"Even before the day begins, I feel like I am already behind."

There was no drama in her tone, only the quiet honesty of someone who had been emotionally stretched for too long.

Her eyes carried the dull heaviness of a person who could not remember the last time she felt mentally light.

"Work has become too much," she continued.
"My head hurts often. My energy is low. And the pressure at home, it does not stop."

This was not about one incident.
Not one heartbreak.
Not one pressure.

It was accumulation. The weight of countless expectations stacking up until her body began to protest.

"I get migraines now, frequently," she said.
"I feel exhausted all the time. My energy is always low."

As she spoke, I could see the fatigue not only in her face, but in her spirit. A recent project shift had shaken her sense of stability at work.

"Since my new role started, I feel mentally drained," she said.
"I procrastinate. I cannot adjust. I keep getting headaches. It feels like my brain has no space left."

She was not unskilled.
She was not incompetent.
She was overwhelmed.

Work demanded emotional presence she no longer had. And when work drains us, the rest of life feels heavier.

For the last five years, she had been navigating the emotional storm of marriage expectations. Proposal after proposal. Discussion after discussion. Hope after hope. Pressure after pressure.

"Every time an alliance fails," she whispered,
"my family blames me. They say I am taking too long, that I am too choosy, that my age is becoming a problem."

She paused, swallowing a tightening in her chest.

"When one match rejected me, I felt broken," she said.
"I started doubting myself, my worth, my future."

It was not just a proposal ending.
It was her family's disappointment, society's expectations, her own dreams, and her fear of time all colliding at once.

She was not afraid of marriage. She was afraid of the shame that follows repeated rejection.

"There is also someone," she said slowly.
"A colleague from a different background. We connect very well. He is kind, steady, supportive. But I feel confused."

Her voice softened.

"I like talking to him. He feels familiar. Safe."

But she knew the realities of her world.

"My family will never accept it," she said quietly.
"They care about caste, status, finances. My emotions do not matter to them."

This was the heartbreak beneath her confusion. Being pulled between who she felt connected to and what her family demanded.

She was living between two worlds. The emotional world she longed for and the practical world she was expected to choose.

"When a proposal checks all the practical boxes, I do not feel emotionally connected," she explained.
"But when someone connects with my heart, I get scared about the practical issues."

This was not indecisiveness.
It was exhaustion.

It was fear of choosing wrong.
It was fear of disappointing family.
It was grief from carrying expectations she never asked for.

Her mind was cluttered.
Her emotions were tangled.
Her energy was drained.

She was not confused. She was overloaded.

When the mind is exhausted, clarity does not disappear; it gets buried beneath pressure.

"You are not weak," I said gently.
"You are carrying too many emotional responsibilities at the same time."

Her shoulders loosened, as if someone had finally named the invisible weight she was holding.

"You are not confused because something is wrong with you," I continued.
"You are confused because no one teaches us how to choose a partner while managing work stress, family expectations, caste pressure, emotional wounds, and fear of rejection all at once."

For the first time, she allowed herself to exhale.

When life places multiple pressures on us at the same time, career changes, marriage expectations, family judgement, emotional fatigue, the mind stops functioning like a decision-maker and starts functioning like a survival system.

We do not think clearly.
We do not feel clearly.
Every choice feels risky.
Every emotion feels tangled.
Every expectation feels heavy.

And when emotional support is missing at home, the burden multiplies.

In partner selection, emotional exhaustion often creates two common patterns.

When someone is practical, stable, and perfect on paper, we feel emotionally numb because fatigue dulls connection. When someone feels emotionally safe, we fear losing family approval or practical security.

This is not confusion. It is cognitive and emotional overload. And overload is not solved by thinking harder. It is eased by support, grounding, and clarity about what truly matters.

She believed she was confused. But she was not. She was carrying too much.

Work expectations.
Family pressure.
Age-related comments.
Caste barriers.
Failed alliances.
Emotional hope.
Practical fear.
Self-doubt.
Loneliness.
And the pressure to make the perfect decision.

What she needed was not urgency. It was space. Space to breathe. Space to think. Space to choose from clarity instead of fear.

And slowly, as pressure softens and self-worth strengthens, she will realise that her confusion was never a flaw. It was her heart asking for time to find what truly feels like home.

Confusion is not weakness. It is the mind buried under too many voices, unable to hear its own. Her story reminds us that confusion often hides exhaustion, especially when expectations from work, family, and society pile up until the heart can no longer choose clearly. When fatigue disguises itself as indecision, the mind bends under pressure rather than lack of strength.

Healing begins when we pause, breathe, quiet the noise, and gently separate exhaustion from truth. The practices that follow are designed to help anyone overwhelmed by work stress, family pressure, or uncertainty in relationships find clarity, balance, and self-trust again. Without rushing yourself into decisions.

HEALING PRACTICES

For Anyone Exhausted by Work Stress, Family Pressure, and Confusion in Choosing the Right Partner

1. Pause Before Making Decisions

Decisions made in exhaustion often turn into regret.
If you feel overwhelmed, give yourself permission to pause.
Clarity grows in rest, not urgency.

2. Separate Fatigue From Truth

When confusion rises, ask gently:
Is this my exhaustion speaking, or my real desire?

You do not need to answer immediately. Awareness itself creates space.

3. Explore Your Core Values

Write honestly about what you want:

What do I want emotionally?
What do I want practically?
What do I want spiritually?
What kind of long-term lifestyle feels right for me?

There are no wrong answers here, only your truth.

4. Create a Partner Alignment Map

Divide a page into two sections.

Emotional needs: comfort, trust, safety, connection.
Practical needs: stability, family openness, lifestyle compatibility.

Look for balance, not perfection.

5. Set Soft Boundaries With Family

You do not need to argue or defend.
Simple phrases are enough:

"I need some time to think."
"Emotional compatibility matters to me."
"I appreciate your concern, and I also need clarity."

Boundaries can be gentle and respectful.

6. Reduce Work Overwhelm With Small Routines

Support your nervous system at work with simple practices such as short work bursts, brief breaks, planning tasks ahead, or slow breathing before meetings.

Small structure creates mental space.

7. Create a Daily Emotional Reset

In the evening, spend about ten minutes with yourself.

Sit quietly for a minute.
Notice your body for two minutes.
Write freely about your emotions for three minutes.
Practice slow breathing for two minutes.
Offer yourself one gentle promise.
Close the day intentionally.

This is not discipline. It is care.

8. Reflect on the Colleague Connection

Ask yourself quietly:

Do I feel emotionally safe?
Do I feel respected?
Is this connection bringing clarity or helping me escape pressure?

Curiosity is more helpful than judgment.

9. Release Age-Based Pressure

Repeat gently:
I am not late. I am evolving.

Your life does not follow anyone else's timeline.

10. Decide When Calm, Not Overwhelmed

You do not need to decide while drowning.
Clarity grows naturally when pressure reduces and self-trust returns.

Reflective Prompt:
Think of one expectation that feels heavy today. What boundary or pause could lighten it?

*****

***"Your vision will become clear only when you look into your own heart."* — Carl Jung**
Clarity comes not from outside pressure, but from recognising our own needs, values, and truth.

CHAPTER TWELVE

When A Loud World Meets A Wounded Child

A young woman with delicate features and neatly parted hair walked in looking composed on the outside, the kind of person others assume has everything together. She entered calmly, but her eyes carried a restlessness that told a different story.

"I don't know why small things shake me so much," she began, her voice quiet but controlled.
"I get anxiety randomly, when I'm working, during presentations, even when nothing is happening."

Her anxiety was not random. It was the echo of a childhood shaped by fear.

When fear is learned early, the body continues to respond long after the danger has passed.

Some wounds do not begin in adulthood. They begin in childhood, in homes where silence hurts more than words and where a child learns to survive without ever feeling seen.

"My parents were abusive," she continued softly.
"My mother had severe mental health struggles. She managed

to take care of herself, but not us. We were just there, unnoticed."

She spoke without anger. What remained was fatigue. The kind that comes from holding memories that were never given space to be felt.

"I was the third girl among four children," she said.
"There was no guidance, no affection, nothing."

Her father was strict, loud, emotionally dominant, controlling, unpredictable, and frightening.

"He never spoke to me with care," she said quietly.
"There was no emotional connection. Only commands. Only criticism. Not just with words, but through the way he treated us."

There was no softness in that home. No warmth. No sense of safety.

"I used to hide when he came home," she whispered.
"I was scared of him. Scared of his voice. Scared of his presence."

She had spent her entire childhood in survival mode, fearful, unseen, unguided, and unprotected.

"My father once told me I was a waste of existence."
She did not say it dramatically. She said it like someone who had repeated the sentence silently for years.

Her childhood was not just difficult. It was emotionally starving.

"There was no empathy. No support. We were on our own."

"I suppressed everything," she said softly.
"All my feelings, all my fears, all my needs. Even today, I don't know how to express emotions."

Now she was thirty-two, married for three years, and the mother of a two-year-old boy. She had built a peaceful life from the ashes of chaos. But the past had not stayed behind.

"My husband is kind," she said.
"But he is loud. Very loud. And pessimistic."

Her body reacted before her mind could.

"When he raises his voice, even casually, I freeze," she said.
"It feels like I am a child again."

Her husband tried to understand. He genuinely appreciated her strength.

"But he cannot fully understand," she added.
"I feel like I am not heard."

Her in-laws did not offer support either.

"During my pregnancy, they did not stand by me," she said.
"They judge my job. They speak in belittling ways. They compare me to their government jobs. I already struggle with inferiority, and this makes everything worse."

The weight of childhood judgment, marital misunderstanding, and in-law criticism had tied itself into a heavy knot inside her.

"I am very scared of being judged," she admitted.
"I feel like a failure because of my past. I am always in survival mode."

She paused, then revealed the coping mechanism that had once protected her.

"I dissociate," she said quietly.
"When things get loud or feel unsafe, my mind leaves the room. I did this as a child when my father shouted or beat my mother."

She had never truly learned safety. She had only learned escape.

"My sleep is disturbed. I have breathing difficulties because I suppress everything," she continued.
"I beg my husband to talk to me, but I don't show vulnerability to anyone. I don't trust easily."

Then she spoke the sentence that held her entire story.

"I don't want to run from my past anymore," she said softly.
"I want to make peace with it."

The child within us never disappears. Loud voices, criticism, and judgment can awaken her even in adulthood. When a child grows up in an unsafe and unpredictable home, the nervous system learns one rule: survive, do not feel. In adulthood, this survival pattern often appears as anxiety, dissociation, fear of judgment, and difficulty trusting others.

Healing begins when we calm the body, name our emotions, and create safety in relationships through gentle communication. The practices that follow are not meant to erase your past, but to help your body slowly relearn safety and give your emotions a language that was once denied to them. Move gently. Healing does not require force.

HEALING PRACTICES

For Anyone Carrying Childhood Trauma, Anxiety, and Fear-Based Responses

When you grow up in an unsafe or unpredictable environment, your nervous system learns to stay alert. These practices

1. Calming the Nervous System With Box Breathing

Breathe in for four seconds.
Hold for four seconds.
Exhale for four seconds.
Hold again for four seconds.

Repeat this cycle six times.

This type of breathing can help reduce panic and gently reset the body when emotions feel overwhelming.

2. Practising Emotional Naming

When feelings arise, try simply naming them.

"I feel scared."
"I feel unheard."
"I feel tired."

Naming emotions helps the nervous system calm by giving feelings a place to land.

3. Gentle Self-Reassurance

When fear surfaces, say quietly to yourself:

These feelings come from my past. But I am safe now.

You are not denying your experience. You are reminding your body where you are today.

4. Grounding During Dissociation

If you notice your mind drifting away, bring yourself back through the senses.

Touch a cold surface.
Press your feet firmly into the floor.
Describe five things you can see.
Listen for three different sounds.
Hold an object and notice its texture.

Grounding reconnects the body to the present moment.

5. Soft Communication With Partners

You do not need to explain everything. Gentle honesty is enough.

"Loud voices scare me. Can we speak softly?"
"I feel overwhelmed and need a moment."
"I am not ignoring you. I am trying to calm myself."

Safe communication builds safety over time.

6. Practising Small Boundaries

Start with simple statements.

"Not right now."
"I need a break."
"I don't want to talk about this today."

Boundaries are acts of self-respect, not rebellion.

7. Giving Yourself Permission to Rest

Rest helps the nervous system heal.

You might allow yourself short breaks, warm showers, time away from noise, soft music, quiet spaces, or moments with something you love.

Rest is recovery, not laziness.

8. Releasing Emotional Pressure Through Journaling

Each day, write five simple sentences:

Today I am feeling…
This feeling may be coming from…
Right now, what I need is…
One small thing that helped me today was…
One gentle reminder I want to offer myself is…

Writing gives emotions a safe place to go.

Reflective Prompt:
Think of one moment today that made you feel unsafe. What gentle reminder could help you feel safe again?

****

***"What is most personal is most universal."* — Carl Rogers**

The pain we keep hidden often connects us to others more than we realise. We are never alone in our struggles.

CHAPTER THIRTEEN

Connection Strained Not Lost

She entered with the urgency of someone who had been arguing just minutes before walking in. She did not come in angry. She came in tired, the kind of tired that settles behind the eyes and does not disappear with sleep.

"I have two teenagers close in age," she said softly.
"A boy and a girl. Both are in higher secondary."

Her voice trembled, not with weakness, but with the strain of a mother who had been holding everything inside for far too long.

"I am trying to discipline them, but nothing is working," she continued.
"Their father supports them in everything, even when I am trying to correct them. So they bypass me. And this morning, we had a fight because of it."

She was not describing a simple family disagreement. She was describing a home where she felt increasingly invisible.

"I am very concerned about my children," she said.
"My daughter has always been average, and that is fine. But

my son was doing well until eighth grade. After that, everything dropped. His marks, his focus, his discipline."

There was pain in her voice, not disappointment, but fear.

"So I put pressure on them. I admit it," she said quietly.
"I ask them to study. I create routines. Wake up on time. Study time. Hygiene. Sleep on time. But they do not want to follow any of it."

Then she spoke the sentence that revealed everything.

"They do not share anything with me now. Whatever I say, they hate me for it."

Her eyes lowered.

"I try to advise them about everything. Food habits. School tests. Social media. Studies," she said.
"But they shut me out. I am worried they are not listening to me at all. I feel tired. Exhausted. Alone."

Her voice broke slightly as she added,

"My son even gives me emotional tension. He threatens to harm himself when he feels overwhelmed. Do you know how much fear that gives a mother?"

Her eyes filled with tears, not from anger, but from helplessness.

"I just want to protect them," she said.
"I want them to have a better life. But it feels like I am the villain in my own house."

As she spoke, I could hear the pain of a woman who was trying, failing, trying again, and failing again, not because she was wrong, but because she was scared.

She was not controlling. She was anxious.

Anxious because she cared.
Anxious because her children were growing up in a world she did not fully understand.
Anxious because she was trying to protect them the only way she knew how.

When fear for a child's future goes unacknowledged, it often disguises itself as control.

And beneath all of it lived the deepest fear of every parent.

What if I lose my connection with my children?

Teenagers are not disobedient. They are overwhelmed. Their brains are going through intense changes, including identity confusion, academic pressure, peer comparison, fear of failure, bodily changes, emotional intensity, a desire for independence, and a heightened sensitivity to criticism.

A teenager's mind often interprets parental fear as pressure, parental advice as interference, parental discipline as control, and parental love as stress.

And when a father unconsciously steps into the role of the friend, agreeing with the children and protecting them from correction, the mother becomes the only one enforcing structure. This makes her appear like the villain, even when she is the one carrying responsibility.

When teenagers feel cornered, they sometimes use extreme emotional statements.

"I will hurt myself."
"I will leave the house."
"I do not care about anything."

Not because they truly mean it, but because they do not yet know how to regulate intense emotions. These statements signal emotional overload, not hatred.

The truth is simple.

Parents push because they care.
Children rebel because they are growing.
Both sides are scared.

And in that shared fear, communication breaks.

"You are not a strict mother," I told her gently.
"You are a worried mother who has been trying to raise two teenagers while feeling unsupported. Your husband stepping in as the friend has left you feeling alone with responsibility, and fear has made you push harder."

She nodded slowly.

"And your son," I continued,
"his words are not hatred. They are distress. He does not yet have the emotional skills to express overwhelm, so it comes out as threats."

Her shoulders dropped as she exhaled, finally understanding that she was not the enemy.

"The connection is not lost," I said softly.
"It is strained. And strained connections can be rebuilt, gently."

She was not a harsh mother. She was a mother afraid of losing her children. A mother who loved deeply. A mother carrying responsibility alone. A mother who wanted her son and daughter to have a life she never had.

And slowly, she began to understand that parenting teenagers is not about controlling them. It is about guiding them with firmness and warmth while learning to regulate her own fear.

Love does not disappear during the teenage years. It hides behind distance, confusion, and growing pains. With patience, safety, and connection, that love finds its way back.

Her story reminds us that parenting teenagers often feels like walking a tightrope between love and fear. What parents intend as protection can feel like pressure, and what children express as rebellion is often overwhelm. Healing begins when parents shift from control to connection, from advice to listening, and from fear to trust. The practices that follow are gentle steps to rebuild communication, restore warmth, and strengthen the bond between parent and child.

Choose what feels possible. You do not need to do everything at once

HEALING PRACTICES

For Parents Struggling With Teen Resistance, Pressure, and Emotional Distance

•

1. Reduce Advice and Increase Listening

Teenagers open up when they feel heard, not corrected.

You might say:
"Tell me what you think. I am listening."

2. Replace Discipline With Collaborative Routines

Instead of enforcing rules, invite participation.

"Let's create a routine together that works for all of us."

Teenagers are more likely to follow what they help create.

3. Respond Calmly to Self-Harm Statements

If a teenager uses intense language, stay calm.

You can say:
"Your feelings feel very big right now. I am here with you. You are safe."

Calm responses reduce fear and increase emotional safety.

4. Create One Weekly Connection Day

Choose one no-pressure day each week.

This could include a walk, a movie, cooking together, tea time, or a short drive.

No discussion about marks, discipline, or expectations.
Only presence, warmth, and shared moments.

Connection must come before correction.

5. Speak With Your Partner Privately

Disagreements between parents should stay away from children.

You might say:
"We need to work as a team. Otherwise, the children will resist both of us."

Consistency builds stability.

6. Choose the Right Time to Talk

Avoid correction when teenagers are tired, eating, studying, angry, or emotionally overwhelmed.

Conversations work best when everyone feels calm.

7. Focus on One Topic at a Time

Instead of discussing many concerns at once, choose one small issue.

Teenagers shut down when they feel overloaded.

8. Offer Choices Instead of Commands

Choices build responsibility and reduce power struggles.

For example:
"Do you want to study now or after a thirty-minute break?"
"Shower first or eat first?"
"Walk or cycle today?"

9. Replace Criticism With Curiosity

Instead of saying, *"You never study,"* try asking:
"What is making studying hard today?"
"What feels difficult right now?"

Curiosity invites openness.

10. Allow Natural Consequences

Avoid punishment when possible. Let real-life consequences teach gently.

Sleeping late leads to tiredness.
Skipping homework leads to teacher feedback.

Life often teaches better than lectures.

11. Praise Effort, Not Just Results

Teenagers need encouragement more than evaluation.

You might say:
"Thank you for trying."
"I noticed you focused for twenty minutes. That is a good start."

Small recognition builds confidence.

12. Avoid Comparisons

Do not compare siblings or children with others, even silently.

Teenagers sense comparison quickly, and it damages self-worth.

13. Model the Behaviour You Want to See

If you want calm speech, speak calmly.
If you want routines, follow your own.
If you want positivity, practice it yourself.

Children absorb energy more than instructions.

14. Shift From Marks to Meaning

Reduce academic pressure by discussing the future, not just grades.

Ask:
"What kind of life do you want?"
"What career feels interesting to you?"
"How can we support your goals?"

The future feels hopeful. Marks feel heavy.

15. Build Small Moments of Warmth Daily

A gentle touch.
A smile.
A shared snack.
A short joke.

Connection grows in small, consistent moments.

16. Do Not Take Teen Words Personally

Teen emotions sound dramatic.

"I hate this."
"You do not understand anything."

These are expressions of overwhelm, not permanent truth. Stay calm. They pass.

17. Teach Emotional Language Slowly

Once a week, ask:
"How was your mood this week on a scale from one to ten?"

This helps teenagers understand their inner world.

18. Keep Conversations Short and Gentle

Teenagers respond better to brief conversations than long lectures.

Two minutes is often enough.

19. Validate Feelings Before Giving Suggestions

Begin with understanding.

"I can see this is hard for you."
"I understand why you feel upset."

Validation reduces resistance.

20. Create an Emotionally Safe Home

Limit shouting, sarcasm, and blame.

Teenagers grow where they feel respected, not controlled.

Reflective Prompt:

Think of one moment this week when your teenager resisted you. How could you respond with curiosity instead of criticism, and connection instead of control?

****

"Empathy is seeing with the eyes of another, listening with the ears of another, and feeling with the heart of another." **— Alfred Adler**
Understanding each other's feelings leads to cooperation, not conflict, especially within families.

CHAPTER FOURTEEN

When the Strongest Person Begins To Change

She came in with a heaviness that did not come from her body. It came from her heart.

"My mother had a major health episode during the pandemic," she began.
"And ever since then, she is not the same. She gets irritated easily, argues with me over small things, and complains a lot. Everything feels sensitive for her now."

Her voice carried worry and exhaustion together.

Before the incident, her mother had been a powerful woman. A single mother who raised her alone. A woman who survived a painful marriage and stood like a shield around her daughter's life.

"She was strong, bold, independent," she said softly.
"We were like best friends. It was always the two of us. She supported me in everything."

Then life changed quietly and without warning.

"We had planned a big celebration after her service," she continued.
"But because of her health, it became very simple. She felt disappointed. And for her milestone birthday, she said she

did not want anything big. So I kept it simple. Now she feels bad about that too."

Guilt flickered across her face, the kind children feel when they love deeply but cannot get it right.

"During her treatment, there was an incident that affected her front teeth," she added.
"She became very insecure about her appearance. Since then, she keeps saying she looks bad and that she has lost her beauty. I do not know how to help her."

Everything her mother once took pride in her strength, her independence, her appearance, her certainty now felt shaken. And the daughter was trying to hold everything together.

"We argue more these days," she admitted.
"I am in midlife now. I get tired too. Sometimes I raise my voice. After every fight, I feel guilty. She feels guilty too. But we cannot seem to stop."

Her voice cracked slightly.

"I want to support her. I want her to feel happy and relaxed. But I do not know what she really wants anymore. I do not know what she is thinking. It feels like both of us have changed."

She paused.

"I need her. She does everything for me. But emotionally, she feels far away."

This was not just a mother and daughter conflict. It was the emotional imbalance that happens when life changes faster than the heart can adjust.

As she spoke, I could hear the grief of two women mourning the versions of each other they once knew. Her mother was not angry. She was scared. And the daughter was not irritated. She was overwhelmed.

Sometimes love becomes tense simply because both people are tired in different ways.

When illness changes a person's sense of self, even love begins to feel unfamiliar to them.

After a major health incident, especially after years of being strong, many parents experience emotional shifts. Mood swings. Emotional sensitivity. Frustration. Insecurity. Fear of ageing. Fear of losing independence. Fear of no longer being the same person.

They rarely express this fear directly. It often appears as arguments, complaints, irritation, disappointment over small things, or a need for reassurance.

And the children who love them feel pressure, guilt, confusion, irritation, and helplessness.

This is not a failing relationship. It is a relationship adjusting to a new chapter.

"You are not doing anything wrong," I told her gently. "You are carrying your career, your home, your responsibilities, and now your mother's emotional world. Anyone would feel tired. And she is not upset with you. She is upset with how much her life has changed."

Understanding softened her eyes.

"She is not disappointed in you," I continued.
"She is grieving the version of herself she once knew."

Sometimes healing begins when we see what is really being lost beneath the reactions.

This was not a story of a mother becoming difficult. It was a story of a mother and daughter trying to find their rhythm again after life shifted in unexpected ways.

Love does not disappear with age or illness. It becomes more sensitive, more emotional, and sometimes more fragile. But the bond between a mother and daughter, even with its arguments and guilt, remains one of life's strongest threads. It stretches, bends, adjusts, but rarely breaks.

Her story reminds us that when the strongest person begins to change, the whole family feels it. What looks like irritation or distance is often grief for a self that once felt familiar. Healing begins when we stop taking reactions personally and start seeing the fear beneath them. The practices that follow are gentle ways to rebuild connection, soften guilt, and create a shared rhythm of care, while also caring for yourself.

HEALING PRACTICES

For Anyone Caring for an Ageing Parent

1. Acknowledge Feelings Before Offering Solutions

Begin with emotional presence before problem-solving.

You might say,
"I understand you feel upset. I am here with you."

Feeling understood often reduces arguments more than explanations.

2. Do Not Take Irritation Personally

Irritation is often frustration with lost strength, independence, or identity, not anger toward you.

Remind yourself quietly,
"This reaction is about their struggle, not my failure."

3. Respond to the Emotion, Not the Complaint

When a parent complains repeatedly, they are rarely seeking logic.

They are seeking comfort.

Instead of explaining, try responding to the feeling behind the words.

4. Create One Small Daily Ritual Together

Simple shared moments rebuild connection.

This could be evening tea, soft music, a short walk, folding clothes together, or sitting quietly.

Consistency matters more than length.

5. Use Calm Boundaries During Emotional Moments

Boundaries can be gentle and respectful.

You might say,
"I want to talk about this. Let us sit calmly and speak slowly."

This protects both of you from unnecessary conflict.

6. Help Them Feel Valued Again

After illness, many parents feel useless or invisible.

Invite their involvement in small, meaningful ways such as choosing a child's outfit, deciding a meal, or sharing stories with grandchildren.

Feeling needed restores dignity.

7. Offer Gentle Reassurance About Appearance

Major illness often brings insecurity about looks and ageing.

Small, sincere affirmations help.

"You look nice today."
"Your smile is still the same."

These words matter more than we realise.

8. Take Short Pauses When You Feel Overwhelmed

Before reacting, allow yourself a brief reset.

A one-minute pause, slow breathing, or a short walk can soften your response and protect the relationship.

9. Share Your Feelings Honestly and Gently

You are allowed to express your longing too.

You might say,
"I miss how close we used to feel. I want us to understand each other again."

Many parents need to hear this vulnerability.

10. Remember That Irritation Does Not Mean Lack of Love

It means both of you are human and carrying change in different ways.

Love often remains, even when patience feels thin.

11. Be Kind to Yourself

You are not only a daughter or son.

You may also be a parent, a partner, a professional, and a caregiver.

You are allowed to feel tired.

12. Build a 'We' Mindset

Shift gently from carrying everything alone to sharing the emotional load.

Instead of thinking,
"I have to manage everything,"

Remind yourself,
"We are learning to adjust to this phase together."

This reduces isolation and softens responsibility.

Reflective Prompt:

Think of one moment when your parent seemed more sensitive than usual. How could you respond with comfort instead of correction, and connection instead of guilt?

*****

"Nothing has a stronger influence psychologically on a child than the unlived life of the parent."

– Carl Jung

When someone loses their old identity or confidence, it affects the emotional atmosphere around them.

CHAPTER FIFTEEN

The Fragile Strength of Motherhood

Her laptop bag hung heavier on one shoulder as she set it down with a long exhale, the kind that escapes only when someone finally pauses after pushing themselves for too long.

"Life feels like a race I cannot catch up with," she admitted. Not just because of work, but because she was trying to be everything for everyone, every single day.

"I have been married for many years," she continued softly. "I have a young son, and I feel like I am failing him every day."

There was no drama in her voice. Only honesty, the kind that comes when guilt has been carried quietly for too long.

"My husband travels a lot for work," she said.
"So most of the time, it is just me, my job, my child, the home, everything."

She paused, as if holding her breath between responsibilities.

"I reach home in the early evening. By the time I come back, my son has already missed that window when children usually play outside. He only gets to join them after I return."

Her voice trembled slightly.

"I enrolled him in classes for his growth, but then I feel guilty again. While other children play freely, mine is in a structured class. I do not know if I am helping him or taking away his childhood."

She was not crying, but guilt sat quietly beneath every sentence.

"I want to be a good mother," she whispered.
"But I am scared I am becoming the opposite. I cannot be there for school activities. I cannot attend everything. I feel like I am not giving him what he deserves."

She looked exhausted, not physically, but emotionally.

"I do not have much support," she added.
"My job requires relocations, so it is hard to depend on my parents. They have their own commitments. I do not want to burden anyone."

This was not just stress. It was loneliness. The loneliness of a mother doing her best while silently fearing she is not enough.

As she spoke, something became clear. She was not failing. She was carrying too much. Many mothers do not break because they are weak. They break because they are trying to be perfect.

Her guilt was not proof of lack. It was proof of love.

When responsibility is constant and support is limited, even love begins to feel like self-doubt.

Modern mothers often live in two worlds. One where they work and build stability. Another where they nurture and guide their child. The space between these worlds creates guilt, exhaustion, self-doubt, and emotional overwhelm.

And when support is limited, the pressure grows heavier.

But guilt does not mean she is doing something wrong. It means she cares deeply.

Children do not need perfect parents. They need emotionally present ones. And she was already giving that.

"You are not doing too little," I told her gently.
"You are doing too much and still judging yourself as if it is not enough."

She looked up, quiet and surprised.

"Your son is not lacking love," I continued.
"He has a mother who thinks of him every single day. Children do not count hours. They feel connection. And he feels that from you."

The relief on her face was soft, slow, and real.

This was not a story of failure. It was the story of a mother who loves her child so deeply that she worries about every small detail.

Children do not remember the guilt their parents carry. They remember warmth, safety, and love.

Your child does not need perfection. He needs you. Your presence. Your listening. Your effort. Your heart.

Her story reminds us that motherhood feels fragile not because mothers are weak, but because they carry too much. What feels like failure is often love disguised as guilt. Healing begins when mothers stop measuring themselves against perfection and start recognising the value of presence. The practices that follow are gentle ways to reduce guilt, restore balance, and strengthen the bond between parent and child..

They are about easing self-judgment and recognising what already matters

HEALING PRACTICES

For Working Parents Who Carry Guilt

1. Replace Guilt With Presence

Even fifteen minutes of undistracted attention builds deeper connection than hours spent together while mentally elsewhere.

Presence matters more than duration.

2. Create One Simple Evening Ritual

A bedtime story, a cuddle, drawing together, or a short walk can become anchors of safety.

Small, repeated moments matter more than full schedules.

3. Separate Love From Time

Children do not measure love in minutes.

They remember warmth, tone, safety, and how they felt with you.

4. Reframe Extracurricular Activities

Classes and routines are not taking away childhood.

They can build confidence, curiosity, and skill when balanced with warmth and rest.

5. Avoid Comparing Your Parenting to Others

Every family has a different rhythm, support system, and reality.

Comparison only creates unnecessary self-doubt.

6. Protect Your Energy

A calmer parent creates more emotional safety than a constantly exhausted one.

Rest is part of good parenting, not a luxury.

7. Let Your Child Guide You Sometimes

Ask what makes your child happiest.

Children often need far less than we imagine and value simple connection most.

8. Reduce Your Self-Expectations Gently

Lower your internal pressure by even twenty percent.

You are already giving more than enough.

9. Share the Emotional Load With Your Partner

Even if your partner travels, speak openly about how you feel.

Guilt grows when carried silently.

10. Remember This Truth

Working parents are not less.

They are strong, loving, adaptive, and resilient.

Your child does not need perfection.
Your child needs you.

Reflective Prompt:

Think of one moment this week when guilt made you doubt yourself as a parent. How could you replace that guilt with presence, even in a small way?

*****

"The good life is a process, not a state of being. It is a direction, not a destination."

– Carl Rogers

Parenting, work, and self-care are continuous journeys; progress matters more than perfection.

SOMETIMES

HEALING

IS JUST A

DIFFERENT

WAY OF SEEING

Conclusion- The Quiet Work of Healing

As you reach the final page of this book, a gentle truth remains:

You made your own journey through these stories and that matters.

Across these chapters we met pain in many forms: childhood wounds, relationships that fray, fears that linger, losses that echo. Yet alongside the pain we also found strength, small acts of courage, and the steady possibility of change.

We cannot change the past. Many things happened beyond our control. But we do not need to punish ourselves or others for what was out of our hands. Instead, we can learn to carry our history with more kindness. Time does not erase everything, but it does give space for perspective, for repair, and for new ways of being.

Healing is not dramatic; it is the quiet accumulation of small choices: a brave conversation, a boundary kept, a gentle breath, a moment of rest, one act of self-compassion. These small acts reshape how we live with our story.

There is a simple wisdom in the work of those who've studied the human heart.
Carl Rogers taught us that acceptance of ourselves and of others opens the door to growth.
Carl Jung reminded us that wholeness comes when we bring light to the parts of ourselves we once hid.
Together, their ideas point to a patient, inward path: accept, explore, integrate.

So carry this with you as you leave these pages:

You do not need to be perfect to deserve peace.
You do not need to erase your pain to build a meaningful life.
You only need to remain open to understanding, to small changes, and to kindness toward yourself.

Even on days you feel stuck, you are moving.
Even when old wounds resurface, there is room to tend them differently.
Even when the path is slow, hope can be steady.

Thank you for reading with openness. Thank you for giving these stories a place to rest inside you.
May the compassion you find here extend outward toward yourself, and toward the people you care for.

The journey continues quietly, honestly, and with the promise that healing is possible.

Author Bio

Gnanambikai Devi R is a counselling psychologist with extensive experience working with individuals navigating anxiety, trauma, depression, relationship distress, childhood wounds, and life transitions. Over the years, she has conducted hundreds of therapy sessions, offering a space where people can speak honestly and feel understood without judgment.

Her therapeutic approach blends humanistic principles, trauma-informed care, and contemporary psychological understanding. Influenced by the works of Carl Rogers, Carl Jung, Sigmund Freud, and modern research, she focuses on helping individuals build self-awareness, emotional resilience, and healthier ways of relating to themselves and others.

She is the founder of **See Thru You(seethuryou.com)**, a platform dedicated to emotional well-being, self-understanding, and mental-health education. Her work reflects her core belief that healing does not require perfection only honesty, compassion, and a safe space to explore one's inner world.

Through her writing, she hopes to make psychological insights simple, relatable, and deeply human, offering comfort to those carrying silent pain and guidance to those supporting them. When not in the therapy room, she continues learning, listening, and reflecting on the quiet stories that shape the human heart.